ANGELS
OF DEATH:
GOERING'S *LUFTWAFFE*

Other books by Edwin P. Hoyt

199 Days: The Battle for Stalingrad
The U-Boat Wars
Defeat at the Falklands
The Kamikazes
The Invasion Before Normandy
Hitler's War

ANGELS
OF DEATH:
GOERING'S *LUFTWAFFE*

EDWIN P. HOYT

A TOM DOHERTY ASSOCIATES BOOK
NEW YORK

ANGELS OF DEATH: GOERING'S *LUFTWAFFE*

Copyright © 1994 by Edwin P. Hoyt

This book is printed on acid-free paper.

A Forge Book
Published by Tom Doherty Associates, LLC
175 Fifth Avenue
New York, NY 10010

www.tor.com

Forge® is a registered trademark of Tom Doherty Associates, LLC.

Library of Congress Cataloging-in-Publication Data

Hoyt, Edwin Palmer.
    Angels of death : Goering's Luftwaffe / Edwin P. Hoyt.
       p. cm.
    "A Tom Doherty Associates book."
    ISBN 0-312-85668-7 (hc)
    ISBN 0-765-30102-4 (pbk)
    1. World War, 1939–1945—Aerial operations, German. 2. Göring, Hermann, 1893–1946. 3. Germany. Luftwaffe—History—World War, 1939–1945.
    I. Germany. Luftwaffe. II. Title.

    D787.H627 1994
    940.54'4943—dc20
                                                94-1455
                                                CIP

First Hardcover Edition: April 1994
First Trade Paperback Edition: August 2001

Printed in the United States of America

0 9 8 7 6 5 4 3 2 1

ACKNOWLEDGMENTS

I am indebted to archivists at the German military archives in Freiburg (Bundesarchiv / Militaerarchiv) for materials about Hermann Goering and the *Luftwaffe,* and also to the librarians of the Imperial War Museum in London. Adolf Galland's *The First and the Last* gave me some feeling for Goering's relationships with his subordinates in the *Luftwaffe.* The Goebbels diaries did the same to illuminate Goering's place in the Nazi hierarchy. Williamson Murray's *Luftwaffe* was very valuable in the study of the German air force. I am also indebted to my editor, Robert Gleason, for the brief sidebars that appear throughout the book.

CONTENTS

ILLUSTRATIONS

PICTURE CREDITS

The Imperial War Museum, London: 1, 2, 3, 4, 6, 9, 13, 15, 17, 18, 19, 26, 27, 28, 29, 30, 31; Ullstein Bilderdienst, Berlin: 5, 7, 8, 10, 11, 12, 14, 16, 20, 21, 22, 23, 24, 25.

GLOSSARY

Geheime Staatspolizei (Gestapo): State security police
Geschwader: Group (air force)
Gruppe: Wing (air force)
Jagdstaffel: Fighter squadron
Kette: Flight (air force)
Luftwaffe: German air force
National Sozialistische Deutsche Arbeiter Partei: The
  National Socialist Workers (Nazi) party
Oberkommando Wehrmacht (OKW): High Command of
  the German Armed Forces
Reichstag: German Parliament
Reichswehr: German armed forces later named
  Wehrmacht
Schutzstaffel (SS): Protection squad; known as blackshirts
Staffel: Squadron (air force)
Sturmabteilung (SA) Storm troopers; known as
  brownshirts
Sturmsstaffel: Assault squadron (air force)
Wehrmacht: German armed forces under the Third Reich

PREFACE

Of all the men who led the Third Reich of Nazi Germany, and especially of all the intimates of Adolf Hitler, one man stands out as a character study of what began as a decent, even outstanding human being, who was corrupted by opportunity and power and who in the end was totally destroyed by events and his own weaknesses. The man is Hermann Gocring, at one time a true hero of Germany and a brave and conscientious warrior of his kaiser, later a flamboyant young man in a decadent Germany, and still later a sycophant of the bloodiest and most devilish dictator in modern times.

More than forty years after Goering's death, his life is still a matter of interest to any who survived the Second World War in Europe and to students of military and aeronautical warfare. For Hermann Goering was a classic example of the man of limited military ability who achieved beyond his depth. As a fighter pilot and commander of fighter pilots in World War I, he had been superb. And when it came to the organization of the German air force in the troubled years when the nation was supposed to have no air forces, Goering's bluff ebullience and World War I reputation served the

cause well. But he was never a first-class strategist or tactician on a major scale. In the end he was probably more
harmful to the German Luftwaffe than helpful; certainly this
was true on the Russian front, where the Luftwaffe wasted so
many of its resources.

Goering's personal tragedy was underlined by his behavior in the dock at the Nuremberg war-crimes trials, where he
conducted himself brilliantly, and often with humor—not so
easy, considering the fact that he knew from the outset that
he was a doomed man. One need not applaud his crimes to
recognize in this once Falstaffian character a tragic figure
and in many ways a victim of the outcome of World War I,
in which he performed so brilliantly.

This book is not a biography of Hermann Goering in the
normal "warts and all" or heroic sense, any more than my
Hitler's War (McGraw-Hill, 1988) is a straight biography.
Both men have their biographers, who have delved into the
personal lives and habits of their subjects. I did not set out
to do this, because in Goering's case his personal life was so
flamboyant that the facts get in the way of understanding
what happened to Germany in World War II and how the
most powerful air force in the world in 1939 could by 1944
become a paper tiger that could not even put up an air
defense over the Normandy beaches.

The fact, of course, is that by 1944 the air war was very low
on the list of Hitler's priorities. What is remarkable about
World War II in Europe is how long the Germans managed
to last, facing the combined might and manpower of the
Soviet Union, the United States, Britain, Canada, Australia
and other British dominions, and those who had left subjugated Europe. A good deal of the reason for that is to be
found in Goering's work as economic tsar of Germany. For,

fault him as we might for his failures as an airman and a general, Goering performed loyally and effectively in creating a German economy that was able to take on the world, and almost get away with it.

1

HERO

Hermann Wilhelm Goering was born in Rosenheim, a little town south of Munich, in January 1893. His father was a former soldier and senior official of the German consular service who had earned a solid reputation in his country's service. Very shortly after Hermann was born, his mother left him, to join her husband and the other three children of the family in Haiti, where her husband was stationed. She had returned to Germany only for the childbirth, having decided that Haiti's climate was unsuitable for a baby.

The Haiti post was an indication that, although Heinrich Goering was respectably employed, he was not a notable

---

THE FATHERLAND

The Germany into which young Hermann had been born was an exciting, vigorous place. The nation, newly united, had begun to feel its strength.
—Ewan Butler and Gordon Young,
The Life and Death of Hermann Goering

figure in the consular service. The Goerings were just that, respectable but not notable; the family had no aristocratic background but was solid middle class, a line of judges, lawyers, and bureaucrats who had hovered around the edges of the German royal courts for generations.

Hermann was left for three years with a family in the Bavarian town of Fürth. He was very lonely and resentful of his parents for deserting him, and when they finally returned to pick him up, he flew into a temper tantrum. Many years later, the *Reichsmarschall* recalled that as a baby he had been very unhappy, and, he said, it was next to a crime for a family to desert a child.

In 1896 Heinrich Goering returned to Germany, to find that his career was in shards; he was forgotten and looked upon with suspicion at the German Foreign Office, because he had long advocated the treatment of black Africans and coffee-colored Haitians as human beings. Soon he retired, to drink himself to death.

Perhaps because Heinrich Goering was so unhappy, his wife became the mistress of Ritter Hermann von Epenstein, a half-Jewish nobleman whose father had been honored because he was physician to the court of Friedrich IV. And a few years after Heinrich Goering's return to a middle-class suburb of Berlin, von Epenstein announced that he was installing them in a castle he had just bought, Burg Veldenstein, built on a cliff overlooking the town of Neuhaus on the Pegnitz River, twenty-five miles north of Nuremberg.

When Hermann was eleven years old, he was sent to boarding school at Ansbach. It was 1904. Having been educated at home until this time, he was a spoiled boy and was quite shocked to be cast suddenly into a school with many others. The school was not a very good one. It was strong on physical discipline but weak on building character, and Hermann was subjected to one great indignity: he was forced to try to learn to play the violin. The experiment was a total failure.

Ansbach was a failure, too. But it brought out one of the best aspects of Hermann's character: loyalty.

One day his class was called upon to write essays. The subject: "The man I most admire." It was obvious that what the teacher was looking for was a patriotic essay on Prince Otto von Bismarck, the German empire builder, or on Friedrich the Great, or at least on one of the kaisers. But Hermann Goering chose to write about Ritter Hermann von Epenstein.

Next morning the boy was called to an interview with the headmaster of the school, who informed him acidly that Ansbach students did not write essays in praise of Jews!

Hermann was indignant. His godfather was a Roman Catholic, he said.

Whatever religion the Ritter von Epenstein professed, said the headmaster, his godfather was a Jew. And he handed the boy a copy of the *Semi-Gotha,* a reference book of the nobility, which very clearly delineated Godfather Hermann's parentage and the fact that his title came from the court of King Friedrich Wilhelm IV of Prussia, where von Epenstein's father had been physician.

Hermann was sent off to write out his penance. "I will not write essays in praise of Jews" was the order.

While he was swallowing the bitter pill, outside on the grounds his fellow students were spreading the word of his disgrace. When he came out of confinement, he was grabbed and held, and a placard was fastened around his neck: MY GODFATHER IS A JEW. He was then frog-marched around the parade ground of the school, while his fellows jeered and laughed at him for making so bold as to praise a hated Jew.

Hermann held in the resentment and the hatred that day, but that night he arose from his bed, packed his belongings, and stole out of the school, first smashing the detestable violin and cutting the strings of all the other stringed instruments in a furious display of his feelings toward school and schoolmates. He took the train back to the family home at Neuhaus.

So Hermann did not go back to Ansbach but to the military academy at Karlsruhe. He was much happier there; it was a good school, and the masters liked boys with verve. Hermann Goering had plenty of that; he was an adventurer. His great love of that period was mountaineering, and he was not afraid of any peak in the world. He climbed Mont Blanc, the Grossglockner, and many another peak before he was fifteen years old.

By the time he left Karlsruhe, he had achieved excellent marks in English, French and history. He was a superb horseman, and somehow, after getting away from Ansbach, he had reacquired a taste for music. But his greatest claim to fame, for which he was praised at Karlsruhe, was his willingness to take any risk offered. The masters liked that.

GREAT PROSPECTS

Goering has been an exemplary pupil and he has developed a quality that should take him far; he is not afraid to take a risk.

—Final report from military academy at Karlsruhe

Hermann was also, at this early age, a hand with the ladies. His sister Paula was going to school at a girls' academy, also in Karlsruhe. One day, in full military outfit, he appeared at the girls' school and descended on the canteen, where many of the students were having a snack. He went round kissing hands, amid many "oohs" and "ahs," until he found his sister.

When Hermann was sixteen, he secured an appointment to the Kaiserliche Kadettenstalt in Lichterfelde, near Berlin, a famous cadet college that sent young men to become officers in the German army. A good record here almost certainly meant a commission.

Hermann fitted in like a hand in a glove. He was soon elected to the most prestigious cadet secret society. The young men comported themselves with great dignity and practiced the chivalry of the past, and the attitude was infectious. Hermann really dreamed of becoming a hero in the Siegfried mold and earning the homage of all Germany.

Life at the academy was very pleasant: hard study and drill during the daytime, but long evenings of beer drinking and girl chasing.

In 1912, Hermann Goering graduated from the Lichterfelde academy. He had been a brilliant student: his record was highest in his class in almost every subject. He was nineteen years old and known as a lady-killer to his fellows. It was true: the ladies loved to look in Hermann Goering's blue-green eyes. In March that year he was commissioned as a junior officer in the Prinz Wilhelm Regiment (the 112th Infantry). The regiment's headquarters was located at Mühlhausen, now Mulhouse in France, and he was posted there. For the next year, he learned to be an officer in the army of the kaiser.

In 1913, his father died, and he went home briefly to attend the funeral and sort out family affairs. Then it was back to Mühlhausen, and the life of the regiment, in which his best friend was Lieutenant Bruno Loerzer. Together they visited the beer halls and went driving in the countryside. Together they drilled their troops in the tradition established by Friedrich the Great.

Mühlhausen is in Alsace-Lorraine, a disputed territory that the Germans had annexed after the Franco-Prussian War of 1870. It was on the west side of the Rhine River, which put it outside the natural defense perimeter of Germany. Therefore, when war broke out in August 1914, Goering's regiment very wisely retreated immediately across the Rhine, with French troops hot on their heels.

Lieutenant Goering, however, did not stay on the German side of the Rhine. That very day he commandeered a train, armed it and moved back onto the French side of the river. The French, in turn, retreated from Mühlhausen in the face of this assault. Goering then led his men into the town, tore down all the French flags and posters announcing that this was again French territory, rounded up four cavalry horses that had inadvertently been left behind, boarded the train and went back into Germany proper. It was not a very significant action, but it was daring enough, and a good indication of the attitude of Lieutenant Goering toward the war and his tasks in it.

The French reinforced the Mühlhausen area against any more incursions, but Goering was not deterred. That second day he led a patrol of seven men back across the Rhine. This time they were riding bicycles, and their intent was to go into Mühlhausen, by the back roads, capture some prisoners and then come out again. They managed to get into the center of Mühlhausen by using roads they knew but most of the

French soldiers did not. They ambushed one French outpost just at dawn. Then they were free to move around.

In the town's central square they spotted a large number of citizens, including the mayor, who were just preparing to greet the incoming French. Goering saw one French officer and sensed that he was the commander, General Paul Pau. Goering decided he would kidnap General Pau and take him across the Rhine. So he prepared to make a lightning dash on his bicycle, up to the edge of the crowd, grab one of the horses tethered there and gallop to the square, snatch the general, who was a small man, throw him across the pommel of his saddle and gallop for the Rhine, with his men behind to cover his escape.

It was a daring plan, and it might have worked, had not one of his soldiers nervously fingered the trigger of his rifle. When it went off, the French jumped, the alarm was given and Goering and his men could do nothing but flee for their lives. They pedaled off toward the Rhine, stopping at another sentry post and capturing four French soldiers, whom they took back to Germany with them. The next day Lieutenant Goering was pleased to see that his name had been mentioned in the command's report of the day.

The German army moved quickly in those early days of the war, but the French and British began to hold, and as the rains of late autumn came down, the battle lines solidified and trench warfare began. Lieutenant Goering's regiment was in the line, and that meant living in dugouts connected by trenches and braving the cold and the damp, which were almost as painful as encounters with the enemy. The Battle of the Marne was beginning. But Lieutenant Goering was not destined for that fight: he developed rheumatic fever and was invalided back to a military hospital in Freiburg im Breisgau. It was a very pleasant place.

As Goering convalesced, he began going into town, to the cobbled square by the cathedral, to sit in one of the cafés and drink beer or coffee and talk. Here one day he ran into his old friend Bruno Loerzer. That officer had transferred out of the regiment just as the war began, to join the new flying corps established by the army. He had been sent to Freiburg to attend the new air training school.

These young "knights of the air," as the press on both sides dubbed the fliers, were the romantic heroes of the new war. War in the trenches was a nasty, dirty job, but war in the air was cool and clean and exciting. The newspapers were filled with the exploits of the fliers. One German pilot had flown around the Eiffel Tower in Paris in September, as the German troops were rushing through Belgium toward the French capital. The names Georges Guynemer and Charles Nungesser were becoming household words in France, just as those of Karl von Hiddesen and Manfred von Richthofen were in Germany. But at that moment the apparent value of the airplane was for intelligence purposes; the aircraft was regarded as the "eyes of the infantry," but the problem was that both sides had those eyes, which complicated troop movements. Pilots tried to intercept and ward off the fliers of the other side as they buzzed across the front lines. They threw spanners, nuts and bolts and rocks at each other. Then they began shooting pistols and rifles, but their aim was not very good. What was needed was a gun fixed to the aircraft, but it would be a few months before such a weapon was devised. At this stage of the war, even bombing from aircraft was little more than a dream.

Lieutenant Loerzer told his friend about his own exploits and his hopes. When he had completed his instruction, he said, he hoped to be transferred to a special aircraft unit that would be stationed at Ostend, Belgium. Its object was to fly across the English Channel and bomb Britain! These operations would be carried out from the forward base of Calais. The problem at the moment was that Calais was still in French hands, and the airmen would have to wait for the ground troops to capture the Channel coast.

Lieutenant Goering decided then and there that he would become an airman, and he wrote off to his commanding officer in France, asking for a transfer to the new flying corps. In the meantime, he began hanging around the airfield where the fliers trained and cadging rides in the observer's seat behind the pilot.

Then came the word from his regiment. The answer was no. He was not going to be allowed to transfer out of the infantry. They needed him in France, and he was to come back to the regiment as soon as the doctors would let him.

Goering ignored the orders. Further, he concealed them and said nothing to the doctors at his hospital. Every clement day he was at the airfield, urging Loerzer and the other pilots to take him up. He wanted to get into action immediately, and there was no way he could get a transfer without his commanding officer's permission, but he could perhaps get taken on as an observer, whose major job was to photograph the enemy troop movements and dispositions with a hand-held camera.

All too soon, his regimental commander learned that Lieutenant Goering had been discharged from the hospital but had not reported back for duty. He was absent without leave, and in wartime this was an offense serious enough to warrant court-martial. His commanding officer was furious and was demanding that Goering be tried.

So Goering pulled political strings. He got in touch with his godfather, the Ritter von Epenstein, and von Epenstein secured a medical certificate which averred that Lieutenant Goering was unfit for infantry duty.

Back in France, the colonel of the regiment had already begun the court-martial proceedings, which could lead to a long prison term or even death before a firing squad for Lieutenant Goering. But in Berlin the Ritter von Epenstein was pulling strings at the kaiser's court and managed to move first. He secured appointments for both Lieutenant Goering and his friend Lieutenant Loerzer from Crown Prince Wilhelm, who was in command of the field air detachment (observation corps) of the Fifth Army.

So the two lieutenants were now to be assigned to the 25th Squadron of the air force. The problem was to get to Stenay, in northeastern France, where the squadron was located, before the military police could arrive at Freiburg, arrest Goering and haul him off to face the mercies of his angry commanding officer. The two solved their problem by going to the airfield, signing up a plane for a flight and then flying the plane to Stenay. They were going to join the Battle of Verdun from the air.

That spring, then, Pilot Officer Loerzer and Air Observer Goering began operations out of the Stenay airfield. They flew a two-seater Albatros low-winged monoplane. It was not exactly designed for air observation. The observer's seat was directly over the wing, so Observer Goering had to do acrobatics in order to take his pictures of the ground. Loerzer would fly the plane to the target and then swoop down low. Goering would stand up in the rear cockpit, brace his knees and feet against the sides and hang over the edge of the nacelle (the framework containing engine and propeller) and take his pictures.

Down below, the struggle for the fortress of Verdun raged. The Germans were besieging the fort. If they could capture it, the flat fields of France lay ahead of them, and the drive to Paris would be easy. But the French were holding out stubbornly at Verdun, and despite the addition of dozens of siege guns to the German forces, the breakthrough did not come. The chief of the German General Staff, General Erich von Falkenhayn, told his fellows that Verdun was the key to the war. He wanted it taken. He knew that the key lay in a whole string of forts in the region, but he did not know much about the forts. He wanted to know everything about them and why the German advance was being held up for so long. The only way to give the staff that information was to take photographs and try to discover the secrets of Fortress Verdun's power. Several aircraft had been sent to do the job, but some had been shot down, and though some had taken photographs, it was from so great a distance that the photos were blurred and unusable by the intelligence officers.

Volunteers were called for, and the team of Loerzer and Goering volunteered. One of the advantages of the little Albatros was its extreme maneuverability. The airmen set out, Loerzer hedgehopping as low as he could manage, and Goering hanging out of the cockpit by his heels, filming for dear life. They spent three days filming. When they returned to the field and delivered the photographs, the army staff were very pleased with the results. The photos were close-ups and they were clear. Crown Prince Wilhelm was proud of his command and of the two young officers. On the spot he bestowed on both of them the Iron Cross, First Class.

Goering decided he needed protection in that backseat. Whenever they flew over the enemy lines, the British and French soldiers below fired at the plane, and their target was the photographer in the back, because they knew he was the dangerous man. So he found a light machine gun and rigged it up in the observer's seat. When he and Loerzer flew low over the ground, Goering would first give the troops at the guns down there a few bursts of machine-gun fire to make them keep their heads down.

The French were pioneers in the next military development of aircraft. One day in April 1915, Roland Garros, a French pilot, rigged up a machine gun on the nacelle of his little aircraft, and shot down an Albatros observation plane. But the problem was that the bullets from the gun smashed into the wooden propeller of Garros' own plane, and he had to make a forced landing behind the German lines. The Germans then had not only the pilot but the plane, and they were more interested in the latter. The aircraft designer Anthony Fokker saw the plane, with its machine gun, and said he could do better. In a week he did do better, having produced a machine gun that was synchronized with the aircraft engine, so that the gun fired between the propeller blades instead of into them.

Thus was born the fighter aircraft of World War I. Hermann Goering was in attendance. One day in May, Fokker, dressed in the uniform of a German army lieutenant although he was a neutral Dutch civilian, appeared at the airfield at Douai, where Goering's squadron was stationed. Crown Prince Wilhelm was there, and so were several other officers. They talked about the new weapon, but the senior officers of the group insisted that it be demonstrated, by Fokker, who must shoot down an enemy plane. Since Fokker was a Dutchman and thus theoretically a neutral, he did not relish the idea—particularly since, if he did this and fell into French hands, his neck would be on the line. He could be shot, guillotined or hanged as a spy.

Fokker went out in his fast single-seat fighter plane, with the gun attached. But nothing happened that day. Several days later he did sight a French two-seater observation plane over the German lines and got it in the sight of the gun, but then he refused to shoot. Why should he fight the Germans' war for them? And so he landed and told the story to the generals. Finally they agreed that a German fighter pilot could do the dirty job. The man chosen was Lieutenant Oswald Boelcke, who was to become one of Germany's great fighter "aces"—meaning he had shot down five enemy planes. This was his first, an unsuspecting victim, who knew nothing of the new weapon. After Boelcke had proved the machine gun, the high command ordered that all pursuit planes be fitted with machine guns.

With this weapon, the Germans became the masters of the air over the western front. But in a matter of weeks the French and the British had responded, having developed their own machine-gun-fitted fighter planes.

The fighter pilot on both sides of the line became the new hero of the war. Max Immelmann (famous for inventing a climbing turn that was used by pilots in three wars), Boelcke and Rudolf Hess all became famous for their exploits on the German side.

Hermann Goering's love of notoriety and excitement drew him to this sort of flying as soon as he saw the results. He would be a fighter pilot, and he would shoot down enemy planes. And so it was back to Freiburg im Breisgau for Lieutenant Goering, this time to take the pilot's course. He arrived there in June 1915. Soon he was as much at home in the air as he had ever been on a mountaintop or the back of a horse. He learned very quickly and within a few weeks led his fellow students in aerobatics and general aeronautical skill. Four months later he was sent to Jagdstaffel 5, a fighter squadron operating on the western front, and there he found his old friend Lieutenant Loerzer again.

But the reunion was not to last very long. Goering was

desperately eager to get into action and prove himself. Three weeks after his arrival at the Jagdstaffel 5 base, he and his squadron were out searching for enemy planes, behind the British lines, when they came upon a heavy Handley-Page bomber, a new invention of the British in this war. The other pilots broke away, because they had been flying in that area for several months and knew that the big bombers did not operate without a fighter escort. But Goering did not know, and he was so eager to fight that he bore in on the bomber. At first he was fired on by the tail gunner and the amidships gunner, but he turned and came back and killed the tail gunner and set the big aircraft on fire.

Then Goering's luck changed. From above he was beset by a flight of British Sopwith fighter planes, machine guns spitting as they came down on him. His plane was hit a dozen times, in the wing and in the fuel tank; then he felt bullets in his thigh. He dropped down toward the ground and nursed the limping plane back out of the British sector, across no-man's-land. The plane sputtered, as the gas ran out from the broken fuel tank. He kept the nose pointed down and tried to glide to safety, but the plane was nearly finished. He saw what seemed to be a cemetery and crash-landed there. It was not a cemetery but a field hospital. Its staff dragged him out of the wreckage of the plane and rushed him to the surgical ward. He was treated there for loss of blood, and bullets and pieces of bone were taken out of his thigh. His life was saved, but it would be a long time before he flew a plane again.

Goering was moved back to a base hospital and kept there for several months. In the summer of 1916 he was sent home on convalescent leave and went to visit the Ritter von Epenstein in his castle at Mauterndorf in Austria, for since his father's death, this was the only real home he had.

In this castle, the war seemed very far away.

2

POUR LE MÉRITE

Lieutenant Goering was soon up and about the von Epenstein castle. He fell in love there, with Marianne Mauser, the
daughter of a rich citizen of Mauterndorf. Her father was not
impressed with the handsome but poor and landless young
lieutenant in his field-grey uniform, despite the Iron Cross at
his throat, but his daughter was enthralled, so Herr Mauser
agreed to a secret engagement—which, of course, in 1915
Germany was no engagement at all as far as the world was
concerned.

With protestations of eternal love, Marianne and Hermann parted in November 1916, and he returned to the
war.

The air over the western front by this time had become a
killing field. Germans and Allies had bettered their aircraft
and their aerial guns to the point at which they were effective
instruments of destruction. The purpose of the fighter squadrons was to protect observation aircraft and bombers going
against the enemy, and to prevent Allied aircraft invading
German territory, but too often the instructions were disre-
garded by young men caught up in the lust of killing and the
urge for fame and glory. One such was the most famous

fighter pilot on the western front, Baron von Richthofen—
"the Red Baron."

Hermann Goering dreamed of being a knight of the air, a
Siegfried whose actions furthered German glory. The air war
was marked by gentlemanly, almost courtly behavior on
both sides. When a pilot was shot down and killed behind
enemy lines, usually during the next day or so an enemy
plane would appear over the pilot's squadron airfield, bear-
ing a wreath with a suitable inscription, attesting his bravery.
If a pilot was captured, he was taken to the squadron mess
of his counterparts and wined and dined regally until it was
time for him to go off to prison camp. But this chivalrous
behavior was not shared by Rittmeister Herr Baron Manfred
von Richthofen. He was a killer, pure and simple, and had
he not been engaged in war, he would have been most happy
as a white hunter in Africa, shooting everything in sight. His
vainglory was such that he arranged with a jeweler to make
for him a small loving cup for each enemy plane shot down,
engraved with the date and the type of plane destroyed. Soon
his trophy collection numbered twenty, then thirty, then
forty and finally eighty.

"One's heart beats faster," he wrote home, "when the
enemy whose face one has just seen goes down enveloped in
flame. . . ."

But most of the German fighter pilots were like the British,
the French and the Americans who would come later, senti-
mentalists at heart, who regarded their calling as a dangerous game. Hermann Goering was certainly cut from this
cloth.

Goering reported for duty on 3 November 1916 to Jagd-
staffel 26. His commander was none other than his old friend
Bruno Loerzer. That very first day Goering was in the air, for
Captain Loerzer was out for blood—two days earlier Oswald

Boelcke, then Germany's greatest ace, had been shot down, and the funeral was being held on this day. To commemorate the event, Loerzer led Jagdstaffel 26 out on a hunt across the enemy lines. They did not encounter any enemy planes.

In the weeks to come, it was a different story. Lieutenant Goering shot down seventeen planes, was awarded two more medals and in the middle of 1917 was given command of a new squadron, Jagdstaffel 27, which was stationed with Loerzer's Squadron 26 at Yseghem in the Flanders region.

Goering and Loerzer remained the best of friends and often fought together in the air. On one occasion, Goering said, Loerzer saved his life when he drove off three French fighter planes that had Goering cornered and had already damaged his plane so that he had to crash-land just behind the German line.

Goering was a tough disciplinarian, but a decent one. On one occasion a pilot reported on a dogfight with a British fighter. The German had gained the advantage and had damaged the British plane so severely that it had to crash-land. The German pilot might have shot the plane down and killed the enemy pilot, but instead he flew above, watching, and when the Briton had landed and jumped out of his wrecked plane, the German pilot rolled his wings, waved and flew away.

"Very good," said Goering. The war to him was made for acts of bravery and gallantry and not of butchery.

The biggest butcher of them all, von Richthofen, continued on his way until 21 April 1918. He had shot down his eightieth plane the previous day, and he was back in the air that morning in his red Fokker triplane, leading the flight of eight other Fokkers on a hunting mission. It was a big day, this aftermath of the squadron leader's eightieth "kill." The regimental band was marching up and down the field as they took off, and von Richthofen was confidently looking for his eighty-first victim.

Half an hour after takeoff, the German squadron was jumped by several squadrons of British Sopwith fighters, and a wide-ranging fight began. Von Richthofen got on the tail of one British plane and chased it down, almost to the ground. Then out of a cloud came another Sopwith, piloted by Captain Roy Brown, a Canadian flying with the Royal Air Force. He got on von Richthofen's tail, fired and hit the Red Baron. The plane turned lazily and began drifting slowly toward the ground. It came down and ground-looped in a shell crater; the wheels tore off and the Fokker slid along on its belly in the field beside a road. The British infantry found the Red Baron, bloody from his wounds, and dead.

DEATH OF THE RED BARON

To the German Flying Corps

Rittmeister Baron Manfred von Richthofen was killed in aerial combat on April 21, 1918. He has been buried with all due military honours.

From the British Royal Air Force

When the word was brought back that the British had buried Germany's greatest war hero with full military honors, the question turned to the future. Who would take over the Red Baron's place as commander of the famous Flying Circus? Everyone expected it would be Wilhelm Reinhardt, who had been named by von Richthofen in his will as the man to succeed him. And so Reinhardt took over. Von

Richthofen's reputation was such that even the high command did not want to interfere.

Air-force headquarters was bemused just then with the coming German offensive on the River Aisne, but in the middle of May the squadron, now named the Jagdstaffel von Richthofen, received orders to transfer from the airfield at Cappy, where von Richthofen had operated, to Guise.

Shortly afterward, headquarters ordered Lieutenant Reinhardt to Alderhof for the testing of several new types of aircraft, including the Fokker D-8, a monoplane. There Reinhardt met Lieutenant Goering, who had come on the same mission. Goering flew the plane, and so did Reinhardt. Then, as they were preparing to go to lunch, Goering spotted another plane, a biplane, parked at one side of the field. It was an experimental fighter developed by aircraft designer Claudius Dornier. Goering said he wanted to fly it. He did, and took it through a wild course of aerobatics. As Goering found the plane extremely maneuverable, he increased the action, until he was giving an exhibition. He landed and walked exultantly toward the canteen. Not to be outdone, Lieutenant Reinhardt took the plane up. He started with a steep climb to three thousand feet. But the aerobatics session just concluded had proved too much for the little biplane, and the left lower wing cracked like a shot and then began to fall away, tearing the upper wing with it. The plane went into a tailspin and crashed. Lieutenant Reinhardt was killed.

Once again the Richthofen Squadron was without a leader. Who would it be this time? The bets were on Ernst Udet, now the leading ace of Germany and a member of the squadron, and he was made temporary commander. But a few days later came orders from the supreme commander of the German armed forces that Goering would command.

WAR HERO

He was now one of Germany's most celebrated pilots. His score of enemy aircraft destroyed stood at twenty-one. In May 1918 the Kaiser recognized the fact by conferring upon him the coveted order "Pour le Mérite." With the award of this distinction young Goering officially entered the Valhalla of Germany's war heroes.

—Ewan Butler and Gordon Young,
The Life and Death of Hermann Goering

The fliers of the Richthofen Squadron were furious. What did it matter that Goering had won the Pour le Mérite, Germany's highest decoration, the Iron Cross with lion and swords, the Hohenzollern Medal and the Karl Friedrich Medal? He was an outsider, and the brotherhood of von Richthofen rejected him.

Goering took command on 14 July 1918. He sensed the resentment from the first. He spoke gently and respectfully to the assembled pilots, praising them as an "illustrious squadron." He promised them his best and said he knew they would do their best—and they cheered him. The crisis was

FACING THE FUTURE

We will need to give our best, all of us, for there are grave times ahead. We will face them together for the glory of the Fatherland.

—Goering upon getting command of air unit

passed. The squadron adjutant, Lieutenant Karl Boden-schatz, so noted in his diary.

The Flying Circus was soon again in action. On this segment of the front, the French were bombing German supply dumps. They used the new twin-engine Caudron bomber, which was protected by armor plate. One day Goering led the squadron out, encountered a flight of these bombers and used up all his ammunition in attacking one, without scoring any results.

The squadron was having problems that disturbed Goering. The pilots had drawn into two camps, one occupied by the "superstars" Ernst Udet, Carl Löwenhardt (who had expected to be made commander) and Lothar von Richthofen, the younger brother of the slain founder of the squadron. These and the other flight leaders kept to themselves and competed for "kills," often disorganizing their flights to go out after an enemy plane. The other pilots of the squadron resented being relegated to an "also ran" position, their effectiveness marred by the antics of the leaders. So one day Goering took the squadron up and made the flight leaders follow him while the seconds-in-command took over the flights. The other flights did very well that day, spurred on by the new opportunity, away from their glory-hunting leaders. Goering led the stars and flew rings around them, charging down on enemy formations, opening them up but then preparing the way for his wingmen to shoot down planes. Only at the end did he single out a British Spad fighter and shoot it down. When the squadron returned to base, its leader told his men that he expected this sort of performance from them from now on. It would be teamwork and no more glory hunting. Overnight the Richthofen Squadron changed, and the result was more effective hunting for the fliers.

Lieutenant Goering continued to believe in chivalry, and

he imbued that concept into his squadron. One day the infantry delivered to the squadron a British officer, Captain Frank Beaumont, a pilot of the British Royal Flying Corps who had been out on a mission that day and had shot down two German planes. In the process his own aircraft had been damaged. He tried to make it back to the Allied lines but failed and was forced to crash-land behind the German front line.

Captain Beaumont spoke excellent German, as Goering and Udet learned when they entertained their prisoner at a banquet that night. The usual procedure called for the squadron to turn the prisoner over to the military police the next day, and then he would be taken to the rear and ultimately end up in a prisoner-of-war camp. But Goering and Udet had taken a liking to Captain Beaumont, and they conspired to keep him at the squadron headquarters for a month before they had to give him up to the authorities. It was a month of toasts and jokes and storytelling, and none of those involved would ever forget it.

In August 1918, Goering turned the squadron over to Lothar von Richthofen and went back to Germany on leave. He went to Munich to visit his mother, and then he went back to Mauterndorf Castle to see his godfather and godmother, and to visit his fiancée, Marianne. But it soon became apparent that the engagement was not going to last, for Marianne's father had begun to show his disapproval of a match with a penniless suitor. By the time Goering left for the front again, he knew that the cause was lost.

That autumn of 1918 the Flying Circus found the going very difficult. The Allies, bolstered by American production, were sending ever stronger formations of planes over the German lines. The Americans were in the war, pouring in aircraft and pilots, and the Richthofen Squadron was running out of skilled pilots, so many had been lost over the months, as increasing responsibility was thrown at them by the high command. In fact, although Goering and his officers did not know it, the whole German war machine was falling apart, and at the end of the first week in October, the German high command was suing for peace through the Swiss government.

The German line began to crumble, and the squadron was forced to retreat back to Tellancourt, a soggy mess of an airfield. But it did not make much difference. A few days after arrival there—November 9—word came from headquarters that air operations were to be discontinued.

On November 10 Goering and his men learned that the kaiser had abdicated and that troops were rebelling all across Germany, including those in Berlin.

When air headquarters also ordered Goering to surrender to the Americans, he refused. He ordered a convoy and the vehicles loaded up to take equipment and men to Darmstadt. The pilots were on the field, preparing to take off, when a staff car came up and an officer handed the adjutant a note demanding that they surrender their planes to the French at Strasbourg. In the end Goering sent five planes to Strasbourg, with orders to the pilots to crash-land the planes so they would be unusable.

But there was another problem. It was a miserable day, cold and rainy, with frequent squalls. Some of the pilots heading for Darmstadt lost their way and landed at Mannheim. As they stopped their aircraft, they noticed a red flag flying over the administration building, and as they walked toward it they were approached by a band of soldiers and civilians. Mannheim, they were informed, was under the control of a Workers' Revolutionary Council. The council quickly took the pilots' guns away and then stripped their planes of weapons. They would be used for the takeover of Germany, the council members said; the navy had rebelled, so had much of the army, and why did not these fliers join up?

The pilots demanded a truck to take them to their destination, and reluctantly it was supplied. When they returned to the field and told Goering what had happened, he was furious. He assembled a flight of planes. Two pilots who had first landed at Mannheim flew there again, and seven others circled the field. On the ground, one pilot approached the revolutionary council.

Lieutenant Goering had ordered that the council make an immediate apology and restore the pilots' personal arms or the seven planes above would attack immediately. They would wait four minutes for the answer. They did not have to wait one minute. The revolutionary council leader took one look at the seven Fokkers circling low above the field and surrendered. He wrote out an apology, the weapons were restored and the two pilots took off in their aircraft.

Goering then led the remains of the squadron to Darmstadt, and he flew his own Fokker there, carefully smashing it up in a ground-loop when he landed.

That night, in the Jagdstaffel day book, he wrote finis to Germany's greatest fighter squadron:

> *11 November, Armistice. Geschwader [Group] flight in bad weather to Darmstadt. Misty. Since its establishment the Geschwader has shot down 644 enemy planes. Fifty-six officers and noncommissioned pilots have been killed, and six men. Fifty-two officers and noncommissioned pilots have been wounded, and seven men.*
>
> *Hermann Goering, Lieutenant*
> *Officer Commanding*

The squadron officers moved down to the old Bavarian city of Aschaffenburg for demobilization. On the night of November 19 they assembled for one last meeting in the dining hall to drink their sorrows away and to spend one last evening in comradeship before scattering to the corners of a Germany rent with revolution. Goering, glass in hand, climbed up on the bandstand and began to speak in a low voice. The room hushed.

He told them of the glory of the Richthofen Squadron, and he sneered at the revolutionary forces that were fragmenting all Germany. He wept as he praised the past glory of Germany. He denounced the revolution and the men who were calling the old soldiers fools and tools of the monarchy.

"No one," he said, "is going to take away our good names, our rights and our freedom, unless we let them."

He wept as he predicted that the Homeland would rise again, and others were weeping, too. Finishing, he drank and then smashed his glass on the floor, and the others solemnly followed.

Hermann Goering, winner of the Pour le Mérite, Germany's highest medal, had just been promoted to captain in a flying corps that no longer existed.

3

DRIFTING

Captain Hermann Goering and Captain Ernst Udet, his most trusted pilot, who had led the five Fokkers to Strasbourg, left for Munich. Goering's mother lived there in a small flat, now that his father was dead and the old love affair with Ritter von Epenstein had burned out. Goering had no job, no money and no prospects.

AFTER THE WAR

In this new, strange, dreadful and defeated Germany, we all felt like aliens and like aliens we clung together.
    —Karl Bodenschatz, upon going home for the first time

He wrote to Marianne, his sweetheart, but had a letter from her father instead.

"What can you offer my daughter?" asked the burgher.

"Nothing," said Goering.

So that was the end of the romance.

In Munich, Goering and Udet joined a unit of the Free

Corps, an organization of former soldiers dedicated to the idea of keeping the German army spirit alive. The group was intensely political and opposed to the ruling group of Bavaria, led by a former journalist, Kurt Eisner. Goering was now involved in work for the Free Corps.

In December he made a trip to Berlin, arriving just in time to attend a meeting at the Berlin Philharmonic Hall called by General Hans-Georg Reinhardt, minister of war in the revolutionary government headed by Friedrich Ebert.

General Reinhardt had issued a call for all former officers to strip the insignia of rank from their uniform jackets and substitute stripes on the arms to show their service. This was the revolutionary way: the Bolsheviks had destroyed all rank in their successful revolution, and the Germans were following. When former captain Goering learned what was expected, he retired to his hotel room, then emerged in full uniform, with captain's insignia and all his medals, the Pour le Mérite dangling at his throat.

When General Reinhardt made his speech to the assembled officers and former soldiers at the Opera House, Goering appeared and walked to the rostrum. He replied to the general's appeal for the officers to join the revolution.

> *For four long years we officers did our duty and risked our lives for the Fatherland. Now we come home, and how do they treat us? They spit on us and deprive us of what we gloried in wearing. I will tell you this, the people are not to blame. . . . No, the ones who are to blame are the ones who have stirred up the people, who stabbed our glorious army in the back and who thought of nothing but attaining power and fattening themselves at at the expense of the people. I ask everyone*

FALLEN HERO

They shouted, "No more war," and tried to tear the decorations from his tunic, as he thrust his way through the press. Only a few weeks before the incident Goering had been one of Germany's heroes. Now the very decorations which testified to his service were a provocation to many of his countrymen. The collapse of Captain Goering's world was almost too painful to be borne, nor was Captain Goering, the war hero, the lover of the good things of life, a man to resign himself to such a catastrophe.

There was indeed little connection between the Germany of late 1918 and the arrogant nation which had plunged Europe into war four years earlier.

—Ewan Butler and Gordon Young,
The Life and Death of Hermann Goering

here tonight to cherish a hatred, deep and abiding hatred, for those swine who have outraged the German people and our traditions. The day is coming when we will drive them out of Germany. Prepare for that day. . . .

Goering's speech was received with great applause by the officers in the crowd, and they carried him out of the hall on their shoulders. But such polemics also gained Goering the attention of the Socialists who were running affairs in Munich, and he began to believe that he was high on a list of people to be assassinated.

Goering's luck held. Udet discovered that one of the officers of the Allied Armistice Commission in Munich, the victors who supervised the dismantling of the German war machine, was Captain Frank Beaumont of the British Royal Flying Corps, the British fighter pilot they had befriended. Now, in 1920, their roles were completely reversed. Beaumont was a high official, with a big house and servants, a car and driver. Goering confided his fears of assassination, and Beaumont helped him escape from Munich and join one of the Free Corps units.

At this point, Goering was sick of politics. Like his friend Udet, he knew only one profession: how to fly an airplane. And both of them found jobs that involved flying. Goering's was an arrangement with Anthony Fokker, his acquaintance from the war years, to test a new Fokker plane, produced at a factory near Amsterdam. This was the Fokker F-7, a monoplane. Goering took it up for aerobatics and made so spectacular a display at an air show in Copenhagen that Fokker saw it would be excellent publicity to have Goering show the plane around Europe. He gave the aircraft to Goering on permanent loan, and Goering now had a job: he moved around northern Europe barnstorming and giving exhibitions of flying skill. He billed himself as the last commander of the Von Richthofen Flying Circus, which did not hurt his image.

During 1919 Goering earned a good living as a pilot, flying, drinking and chasing girls. But after nearly a year of this he was tired of it, and the dangers were coming home to him. One day in a stunt festival he ripped off the undercarriage of his aircraft and had to crash-land it. So in 1920 he applied for a job with a Swedish airline. While he waited, he put his plane into service on a charter basis.

One day a Swedish nobleman, Count Eric von Rosen, missed his train from Stockholm to Lake Baven, where his castle was located, and went to the airfield to secure transport. It was a dark, gloomy day with snow forecast for the north, and three pilots on the airfield turned the count down. Finally he came to Goering. He offered to pay double the normal rate, and Goering accepted.

They took off and almost immediately got lost in the bad weather but picked their way up through the lake country until they arrived at Lake Baven, in the midst of a snowstorm. Goering landed on the ice, tied down the plane and accepted the count's invitation to spend the night at the castle.

The medieval castle was filled with bearskins, and a large stuffed brown bear stood at the head of the great staircase—an animal killed in the old fashion, with a hand-held spear, by the master of the castle. A fire burned brightly in the fireplace of the great hall, which was festooned with ancient weapons and with two large swastikas adorning the huge andirons.

There, in the atmosphere of Valhalla, Goering met Carin von Kantzow, the thirty-two-year-old sister of the Countess von Rosen. Carin was the wife of Nils von Kantzow, a soldier in the Swedish army, and she had an eight-year-old son named Thomas. She was restless, she did not love her husband and she was, according to her sister, looking for a hero, a Siegfried who would quicken her blood.

And here, in the castle, before the great fire, she found Hermann Goering, aged twenty-seven, and she listened as her brother-in-law drew him out to tell about his war experiences.

The evening was emotional. The count drank a toast to the future of Germany and to the day when she would find a leader who would make her free again—and suggested that

Goering might be that man. The count then brought out a lute and began singing songs from the days of the Vikings.

Soon Goering was invited to lunch at the Kantzow house. They began meeting at Carin's parents' house, and it was not long before she told her family that she intended to leave her husband. Soon enough she did: her son was sent to stay with the von Rosens, and Carin and Goering moved into a flat in Stockholm. She took him to art galleries, exhibitions and museums and brought to him a cultural appreciation of the European Old Masters that was to last all his life. But in the early summer of 1921 Goering was bored with life in Stockholm. He was a German, and he was getting nowhere by staying in Sweden. So he returned to Germany.

Goering's mother had managed to secure entrance for her distinguished son to study history at the University of Munich. Carin von Kantzow followed a month later. Soon she returned to Sweden and got a divorce. She and Goering were married in Munich City Hall on 3 February 1923.

At the University of Munich, Goering met many old soldiers like himself who believed that they had been let down by their government. His feeling of shock and disappointment at the outcome of the war was easy to share; he and his fellows talked about it endlessly in the cafés. The German people had gone to war expecting victory, and the propaganda from their leaders had never indicated that there was any possibility of surrender. Therefore, when the armistice signed in the Forest of Compiègne was followed by the Versailles treaty talks, at which the French said quite flatly that they were going to punish Germany, they were met by the indignation of the old soldiers and now of the students at what they saw as the cupidity of their leaders. The insatiable demands of the Allies for reparations were sapping the German economy, and this also sat badly with the public. The inflation that was superimposed on the country by the government, seeking to pay its war debts, wiped out the middle class.

NO IDLE THREAT

One day we will write another treaty.
— Goering in 1919 about the Treaty of Versailles

Like others he knew, Goering began to use such words as *traitor* and *scoundrel* to describe the members of the government that had lost the war, and those men who were administering the German economy in the 1920s.

Disillusioned, poor and without any clear vision of a future, Goering was fumbling for something in which he could believe.

At this time political feelings in Germany ran very high. A number of nationalistic groups were springing up across the country, most of them dedicated to stamping out the results of the Versailles treaty and throwing out of office all the political leaders who had had anything to do with the ending of the war and the early administration of the peace. The anti-Semitism that had so shocked the young Goering at his first boarding school was now commonplace among the German people; so many of the political and industrial leaders of the bad days were Jews. The Völkische Verbände (Nationalist Groups) were dedicated to racial purity and to anti-Semitism.

And then Goering met Adolf Hitler, the leader of the National Sozialistische Deutsche Arbeiter Partei (National

Socialist German Workers' party—the Nazi party), which considered itself to be the left wing of German politics, different from the Communists because it was intensely nationalistic but sharing the Communists' distrust of parliamentary procedures and their strong desire for revolutionary action.

Goering and Hitler talked for a long time. They agreed that Germany had been "stabbed in the back" by the leaders who surrendered the country in 1918 and permitted the Versailles treaty to rob Germany of her resources and territory to the east, and all her colonies overseas. Goering agreed that a new Germany must be built and that the Versailles treaty must be refuted somehow. At first the one sticking point for Goering was Hitler's attitude toward the Jews, whom he lumped with the Communists as the mortal enemies of Germany. Goering had never felt that way in the past but now, enchanted by Hitler, he swallowed the anti-Semitic line.

DEMOGOGUE

As Goering had discovered on hearing him speak for the first time, Hitler was a spellbinder whose skill with words not only roused to fever heat those who heard him but kept them on the boil long afterward.
—Leonard Mosley, *Reich Marshal*

He took Hitler's hand and said, "I pledge my destiny to you for better or for worse. . . ." He vowed to give his life if necessary in support of Adolf Hitler. And he emerged from the meeting as a man with a cause. His days of drifting were behind him.

SUDDEN LOYALTY

Until men learn a great deal more than they at present know about the human mind, it is unlikely that any very satisfactory explanation of the sudden affinity that Goering felt that afternoon for Adolf Hitler will ever be given. Goering himself could never explain it save in vaguest terms: "All at once, I felt instinctively that there was a Leader whom Germany needed."

4

THE REVOLUTIONARY

What sort of man was this Adolf Hitler on whom Hermann Goering pinned his hopes in the autumn of 1922?

He was an intense man of compelling presence when he spoke in public, and his piercing eye showed that his words were a true representation of his innermost thoughts. From boyhood Adolf Hitler had dreamed of the unification of all the Germanic peoples. He was Austrian by birth, but that had never prevented his feeling that Germany was the Motherland. A young manhood spent in bitter disappointment had given him a hatred for people with money, for Communists and for Jews. Many of the people he had seen in gilded carriages around the Ring in Vienna had been rich Jews. So had many of the trade-union officials and Socialists with whom Hitler argued in the Vienna cafés as he tried desperately to find a career as an architect or artist and ended up working with construction crews. So that aspect of his bitterness was very personal and very deep.

Hitler was in Munich when war broke out in Europe. He enlisted in a Bavarian regiment as a common soldier and during the war comported himself with bravery, winning the Iron Cross and mentions for gallantry, and conceiving a strong dislike for the Prussian generals and the war's leadership. When the war ended in failure and ignominious surrender at Versailles, Hitler's reaction was fury at the men who had "betrayed" Germany. This emotion was shared completely by Hermann Goering and millions of other young Germans.

"TO HELL WITH VERSAILLES"

I joined the Party because it was revolutionary. Other parties had made revolutions, so I thought I could get in on one too, and the thing that attracted me to the Nazi party was that it was the only one that had the guts to say, "To Hell with Versailles."

—Goering

Hitler sensed the strength of his argument. What he needed was a vehicle, and he found it early in the 1920s in Munich, in the National Socialist Workers' party, a radical party whose major tenets included the overthrow of capitalism, the Jews and supernationalism. Within a matter of months, he had tailored the party's concepts to his own.

In the autumn of 1922 he was looking for adherents who had strong connections or associations that would help strengthen the party among the German people. That is why Hermann Goering appealed to Hitler so much: Goering was young, undeniably Aryan with his blond good looks; his war record was superb, with the Pour le Mérite and the name of von Richthofen behind him. It was the sort of record that would appeal to other old soldiers and high officers as well, for in spite of Hitler's contempt for the Prussian generals, he needed them just now, and he was never above a compromise that would further his own ends.

PUBLIC ICON

Yet now all this might, Hitler hoped, be retrieved, for in Captain Goering he had perhaps found the key which might open for him doors hitherto stubbornly bolted against the National Socialists.

His birth, glamour and decorations would serve to impress both the potential friends, whom Hitler sought to influence, and the raw recruits who, under Goering's leadership, were to be moulded into a body of fanatical political soldiers.

—Ewan Butler and Gordon Young,
The Life and Death of Hermann Goering

Hitler had settled down in Munich because he had ended up there in the army, finally working as an organizer for the new army but looking more for his own best chance. By 1923 he had control of the Nazi party and had attracted several thousand people, mostly old soldiers, to his banner.

By the summer of 1923 the Nazi party consisted of thirty-five thousand people in Munich and an estimated hundred and fifty thousand in all Bavaria. Most of these intensely nationalistic parties of Germany had their own little police forces—or gangs of bullyboys, depending on how one looked at them. The Nazis were no exception. Soon Hitler had developed a force of about five thousand young men, whom he called Sturmabteilungen (SA, storm troopers), the name derived from the commando-type units that had fought bravely for Germany in the war. He gave Goering the command of the SA, with the order to double, triple its size and make it an effective force. But effective for what? To protect the meetings at which Hitler raged against the Jews and the capitalists and the government and to break up the meetings of competing parties.

In less than six months after joining the Nazis, Hermann Goering had made an effective small army. The men wore brown shirts, breeches and jackboots, and they had a black band with a white swastika on it tied around their arm. They paraded on Sundays in towns and villages around Munich, and became noted for their marching and their tight discipline. All this was Goering's doing. He had imbued these men with his own sense of destiny. He had made them take the oath of fealty to the SA again, even though they had taken it before: "I promise to see in every member of the Sturmabteilung 1, without thought of class, occupation, wealth or poverty, only my brother and comrade. . . ."

THE FÜHRER'S FAVORITES

Adolf Hitler was overjoyed at the transformation of the units he saw passing before him through the Munich streets, and when it was over he slapped Hermann Goering on the back and kissed Carin's hand.
—Leonard Mosley, *Reich Marshal*

And so the SA became a "band of brothers" pitted against all the other semimilitary organizations that thronged Bavaria, and often clashing with the Socialists and the Communists. Goering's house in the suburb of Obermenzing became the center of the Nazis' social activity, and Carin Goering became the hostess of the party. Hitler spent many evenings there, talking while others drank and smoked, planning and organizing for the future. Around him gathered the nucleus of the party faithful, some of whose names would later be famous and infamous in the world: Rudolf Hess, another famous fighter pilot; Alfred Rosenberg, the "philosopher"; Captain Ernst Röhm; and Ernst Hanfstängel.

They sang and they shouted and they drank toasts: "To the devil with Versailles!"

In fact, Ernst Röhm was Goering's rival. He had worked his way up to a captaincy through the ranks of the army, and he hated the Prussian officer class; indeed, he brought fuel to Hitler's distrust of the generals. Röhm wanted to be running the SA himself, but Hitler decreed that Goering should be the commander, and Röhm had to be content to be chief of staff. He dreamt of the day when he would use the SA to form a whole new German army.

In 1923 the organization of the Nazis prospered, and Hitler began to make more ambitious plans. There lived in Bavaria one of the most famous of German generals, Erich Ludendorff, a member of the General Staff and chief of operations until he had refused to recognize the staff's bid for an armistice and been fired from his job. The dismissal had made him a hero when Germany was known to be defeated, and so had his participation in the Free Corps movement, attempting to put together a military force that could bring revolution to the country. All these efforts had failed in 1920, and Ludendorff had fled to Bavaria to escape the anger of the Weimar Republic. He lived in a villa in the village of Ludwigshöhe, near Munich, with a small but powerful armed guard. Through an ardent female member of the Nazi party, Mathilde Kemnitz (whom he later married), General Ludendorff was drawn into Hitler's circle.

The Nazis also met at a public house near the Frauenkirche. Hitler was usually there, but Goering almost always. Röhm came, with his chief bully, Edmund Heines. Goering, Hess and Hanfstängel were the intellectuals. Dietrich Eckart was the editor of the *Völkischer Beobachter,* the party newspaper. They called the place Bratwürstglöckle—"the sausage assembly"—and there they talked politics and drank beer and sang patriotic songs.

Into this fraternity General Ludendorff was drawn by Mathilde Kemnitz, but whether his fascination was for the party or for her was not quite clear. In any event, the doddering general soon convinced himself that Germany had been betrayed in any number of ways and that Adolf Hitler and his brownshirts (the SA) were the wave of the future.

In January 1923 the French government gave Hitler a weapon for the future. The French had never forgiven the Germans for their defeat in the Franco-Prussian War and for the destruction of nearly a whole generation of young men in the 1914–18 war. Four years after the Versailles treaty they were as full of hatred as ever, and when the Germans failed to live up to the letter of the reparations-payment arrangements that winter, because of very hard times in Germany, the French marched into the Ruhr Valley, the industrial heart of Germany, and took possession of it. Ostensibly the action was taken to speed production of reparations materials; actually it was a move to humiliate the Germans further, and it was carried out by black French colonial troops, much to the fear and disgust of the Germans.

The move was made for Hitler. He fulminated against the French in the beer halls, and the *Völkischer Beobachter* screamed against them in its columns.

The French occupation of the Ruhr was the last straw on the pile of oppression that had weighted down the German economy. The German mark fell from fifty thousand to the pound sterling to twenty million to the pound in six months. The middle class, which had been staggering under the economic burden of reparations, faced complete extinction. The membership of the Nazi party swelled, and Hitler, Goering and the others came to the conclusion that it was time for them to strike a blow and take power in Bavaria, and then perhaps in Germany.

By this time General Ludendorff had joined the Nazi party. He and Hitler and Goering conferred, and then Ludendorff went to see General von Lossow, the commander of the army troops in the area. Goering gained the definite impression from Ludendorff that von Lossow would either help them in their attempted coup or stand by and let it happen.

So Hitler planned a putsch—a seizure of power.

That summer the Germans in the Ruhr offered passive resistance to the French, and the French threatened reprisals. That action brought thousands out to a Nazi rally at Nuremberg where Hitler pledged a campaign against "Marxism, internationalism, pacifism, the Weimar constitution, international capital and the Jews." Thousands cheered.

But the Nazis were not the only force in motion that summer. The Communists and the Socialists were also pressing for support, and so were other right-wing groups. A movement calling for the secession of Bavaria from Germany and creation of a kingdom of South Germany took hold. General von Lossow, the army commander in the area, was said to be supporting it, and so was the chief of the Bavarian police, Colonel von Seisser. The head of the movement, Ritter Gustav von Kahr, said he would put Prince

Rupprecht of Bavaria, son of the exiled King Ludwig, on the throne of the new state. All this would be proclaimed at a meeting on 8 November 1923 at a beer hall in Munich called the Bürgerbräuhaus.

Carin Goering was very ill with a respiratory infection and was confined to bed, but this did not stop Hermann Goering from his furious political activity. On November 8 he was ready.

The proposed meeting had attracted the attention of many political groups, and on that evening the beer hall quickly filled up, so that more people were outside than in. Hitler was there, sitting at the back behind an untouched tankard of beer, listening to the Bavarian band that opened the ceremonies.

With him were Hess, his secretary now; Max Amman, the business manager of the Nazi party; and his bodyguard, Joseph Gerum.

The meeting began. Gustav von Kahr arrived, with General von Lossow and Colonel von Seisser, and they ascended the rostrum. Von Kahr began to speak.

Just then, a truck screeched to a stop outside the beer hall, and armed men with steel helmets began pouring out. To the bystanders they were soldiers of the Reichswehr, the German army; in reality they were SA chief Hermann Goering and his bullyboys. Someone informed Hitler, and he rose from his seat and threw his tankard on the floor. He and his companions drew pistols and began waving them as they moved toward the stage. Outside, Goering and his men brandished their arms and moved into the beer hall.

The Nazis had a hard time pressing through the crowd toward the podium, and it was several minutes before von Kahr was aware of them. His voice trailed off and he looked blankly at the approaching men with guns.

One of Colonel von Seisser's aides had his hand in his pocket. Hitler threatened him with his pistol, putting it against the man's head. He took his hand out of his pocket. It was empty.

Everyone began shouting and moving. Goering jumped up on a table and kicked away the beer tankards, which went crashing to the floor.

"Silence!" he shouted.

No one paid any attention. The hubbub increased.

Hitler fired a shot into the ceiling. "If you are not quiet, I will have a machine gun brought in."

The crowd suddenly hushed. Hitler began to speak. He had no quarrel with von Kahr and his people, he said, but this was not the way to go about changing matters in Bavaria. First a new government must be formed, and it must consist of General Ludendorff, General von Lossow, Colonel von Seisser and Hitler.

Von Lossow and von Seisser were dumbfounded. This was the first they had heard of such a scheme. The crowd swiftly assessed Hitler's words and found them welcome. Men began to cheer. In five minutes Hitler had the beer hall firmly behind him.

Hitler then took the four men on the podium into an anteroom. He displayed his pistol and threatened them. Then he went back into the beer hall and told the crowd that the count, the general and the colonel were discussing matters. Would the crowd support the revolution?

His voice was drowned out by the cries of affirmation. But he shouted: "Either the German revolution begins tonight or we will all be dead by dawn."

Goering sent a man into the anteroom, a man armed with a submachine gun. Then General Ludendorff arrived, his dress uniform covered with medals and gold braid. He went into the anteroom, charged by Hitler to talk the others round. And he did, or the machine gun did, for soon they all emerged and announced that they would work with the Nazis to carry forth the revolution.

The band began to play. Waitresses came out with beer and sausages. The conspirators, Hitler, the count, the general, the colonel and Ludendorff, stood on the stage and beamed as the crowd milled about congratulating them. Goering went around congratulating his storm troopers. So the evening ended in triumph, and Hitler and his Nazis looked forward to control of Bavaria and then of Berlin.

HITLER'S DREAM

The day for which I have waited with such longing has arrived. I will make of Germany a glorious State!

—Hitler

Hitler was confident, but as a measure of caution he ordered the SA to seize a number of prominent citizens of the town, bankers, industrialists and politicians, and hold them as hostages to the revolution. It was just a matter of insurance, he said. They had the word of von Kahr, von Losslow and von Seisser that the revolution was a success.

But it was not to be so easy. Von Kahr, von Lossow and von Seisser left the beer hall at about midnight, when the party broke up, but they did not go to their homes. Von Kahr fled to Regensburg, where he proclaimed the kingdom of Bavaria, with himself in charge. Von Seisser went to his office, and von Lossow went back to his army headquarters, where he found a message from General von Seeckt, the commander in chief of the German army in Berlin, warning him that he must put down the rebellion or von Seeckt would come with troops.

The next morning Hermann Goering awoke to learn that all three had denounced the agreement with Adolf Hitler and Ludendorff and that Munich was full of armed troops, with more coming by train. The newspapers were full of accounts of the rebellion and of the reactions of the three dissidents.

The majority of the people, it seemed, were on the side of the rebels. They avoided the troops or cursed them, and they cheered Hitler. But Hitler and Goering knew that without the support of the German army the revolt was in trouble, and if the army intervened, the day was lost.

When Hitler suggested that Goering's storm troopers retreat toward Rosenheim, in the south, Ludendorff was scornful. He told Hitler that they must go ahead, march on the city and take control. The soldiers, he said, would respond to his leadership as they always had. And Hitler believed him, because the old general was one of two whose reputation with the ordinary soldiers had survived the debacle of defeat in the war. The other was von Hindenburg, who would soon become president of the Republic.

So the storm troopers and all the Nazi party faithful and the party's followers massed on the bank of the Isar River outside Munich and prepared to march into the city and take control. Then Hitler had another idea. He told Goering to mass the storm troopers in the beer hall once more, and there, under the eyes of hundreds of spectators, they swore a solemn oath to support General Ludendorff as head of the new government. They marched out of the Bürgerbräuhaus then, into the square, and formed into a column.

At a signal from Goering, the parade began, led by a brownshirt officer carrying a huge red, white and black swastika flag. Behind came a phalanx of SA men, rifles slung across their shoulders. And behind this squad came Adolf Hitler on the right, General Ludendorff in the center, and Hermann Goering on the left, with their aides packed in behind them. After them, surrounded by storm troopers, came the hostages they had taken the night before. Hitler and Ludendorff were fully confident, but Goering was quite sure that the German police and the military would try to stop them.

The column halted at the Ludwigsbrücke, the bridge that crosses the Isar River. On the town side stood a unit of Bavarian police, rifles raised, warning them not to attempt to cross over. Goering went forward to speak to the commander of the guard. He pointed to the hostages and warned the lieutenant that, if the police opened fire on the storm troopers, the hostages would be shot. The police backed off and the column filed by them. Hitler sent the hostages back to the beer hall for safety.

The storm troopers crossed over the bridge and into the town, reached the Marienplatz and walked up the Residenz-strasse. Ludendorff wore a broad smile. The men behind were singing. The crowd was waving and shouting in praise of Ludendorff and Hitler. The column marched down the Residenzstrasse, toward the Odeonsplatz at the end, but there, blocking the narrow street that let into the square, was a column of police.

One of the Nazis stepped forward and told the officer not to fire, because General Ludendorff was in the van. But the officer had been told by Colonel von Seisser that the Nazi column was not to be allowed to pass, and so he ordered his men to open fire.

Max von Scheubner-Richter, who was marching alongside Hitler, fell with a bullet through the head. He bumped Hitler as he fell, and Hitler went down too. Goering was hit in the groin. The police fired again, and the Nazis fired back and then fell back. General Ludendorff continued to march forward, head held high. He marched into the open arms of the police, who surrounded him and arrested him.

A small car came up and rescued Hitler, who had dislocated his shoulder in the fall. Goering was bleeding from his wounds in the groin and the hip. He was picked up by some of his SA men and taken to the house of a furniture dealer named Ballin, a Jew, whose wife treated his wounds. He was kept there, hidden from the police, until night, when he was taken to a clinic in the city.

Back at the Odeonsplatz the casualties were counted. Three policemen had died, and so had sixteen Nazis. Hitler was in hiding and would be arrested in a few days. Goering was in despair. What would the Nazis do now?

Goering was moved to a clinic, and Carin came from her sickbed to be with him. The search was on for the Nazis. He was taken by car out of Munich to Garmisch-Partenkirchen, sixty miles to the south. He stayed there two days, but when the word got out that the famous Hermann Goering was in town, crowds began to gather outside the villa, and Carin became so worried that she insisted they cross the frontier into Austria. But at the border Goering was arrested and taken back to Garmisch-Partenkirchen, where his passport was confiscated. He gave his word not to try to escape, but Carin pointed out that the people to whom he gave his word had already broken their word to the Nazis, so it was meaningless. Goering was convinced by this specious logic and agreed to escape. Friends got him a fake passport, and so they escaped from Germany and went to Innsbruck.

Soon Goering was in touch with other Nazi leaders in Austria and with Hitler in Germany, but there was a price on his head, he had very few resources and his wounds had become infected. They were weeks in healing, and in that period he was given morphine injections for pain. By Christmas he was on the mend and moved into a hotel.

Hitler was about to go on trial. Goering thought he ought to cross over and join the other German Nazis, but Hitler said he must remain in Austria, so he did. He watched as the Nazi party grew in power and influence, winning seats in the Reichstag in Berlin. He saw von Kahr resign from politics, von Lossow fired as head of the army in Bavaria, and von Seisser become an object of contempt in Munich.

Goering's main task was to raise money for the party in Austria. This activity brought him to the unfavorable attention of the authorities, who suggested that he ought to move on to another jurisdiction. After the conviction of Hitler and Hess (who were sentenced to five years' imprisonment in a fortress), he went to Italy. His wounds were still stiff and painful, and he had in fact become addicted to drugs. Using them, he was able to function.

Goering had an appointment with Benito Mussolini, the Italian dictator, but nothing came of it. He also found that Hitler had forgotten him during the period of his imprisonment. Hitler's mind had been on his manifesto, *Mein Kampf,* which he dictated to Rudolf Hess. When he came out of prison, in 1925, he found the party a shambles, with Alfred Rosenberg, the philosopher, in charge. Rosenberg and Goering had never got on, and in Hitler's absence Rosenberg had ejected Goering from the party. Hitler rectified this, but he did not seem much interested in Goering's troubles.

Goering and Carin went to Sweden, where her health deteriorated and he became so violent when trying to shake off the morphine habit that he was put in a straitjacket and declared insane.

By drastic means he managed to shake the habit, but as

AMONG THE MADMEN

He was taken to Langbro Asylum for the Insane on September 1, 1925, and spent the next days racked by the horrors of deprivation in a padded cell.

The psychiatrist who dealt with his case at Langbro Asylum was afterward to classify his patient as "a sentimentalist lacking in basic moral courage."

—Leonard Mosley, *Reich Marshal*

---

soon as he was released from the hospital he went back to it. A second attempt cured him, however, and he never again took morphine.

But in 1926, when Goering recovered from his addiction, he was a changed man. The wound and the morphine addiction had done something strange to his glandular system, and he grew fat. He was thirty-three years old, but he looked forty. Yet the old restlessness was still there, even in pain, and he decided it was time for him to be getting back to Germany and to political life.

The problem was that he was a fugitive from justice. That was rectified in 1927, when the Reichstag's extremists banded together—left and right—to help pass an amnesty for all accused of political crimes. Hermann Goering was free to return to Germany.

Field Marshal von Hindenburg was elected president of the Republic, and in 1927 he presided over what is called "the Tannenburg Demonstration," an outburst of patriotic fervor joined in by millions, and really a loud protest against the Treaty of Versailles and all that had happened to Germany since that time.

"The accusation that Germany was responsible for this greatest of all wars we hereby repudiate. Germans in every walk of life unanimously reject it. . . . With clean hearts we marched out to defend our Fatherland and with clean hands did we wield the sword. . . ."

All Germany cheered, and so, in Stockholm, did Hermann Goering when he read the reports in the morning newspapers. He knew the time had come for him to go home.

5

POLITICIAN

A lone Hermann Goering took the train from Stockholm to Berlin one day in October 1927. He and Carin had decided it would be best for her to remain with her relatives, while he reestablished his connections in Germany. He did not know that the real reason she was remaining behind was that she was mortally ill with tuberculosis.

When Goering arrived in Berlin, he found a new Germany and a new Nazi party. The party he had left had been a revolutionary organization, small, tightly knit and without much electoral power. In 1927 the party was strong and had a large following in Germany. Hitler was no longer a little demagogue surrounded by a handful of sycophants. The old days of comradeship when the whole gang would gather at the Goering villa and swap stories over beer were long gone.

Hitler had great aspirations to control the government that under von Hindenburg was suddenly so much more amenable to his approaches. Many of the old faces were gone: Goering's job as leader of the SA had been taken by a man named von Pfeffer. Goering journeyed to Munich, where he found a bustling Nazi party and a Hitler who seemed too busy to pay much attention to his former comrade. But there was a real reason for Hitler's coolness. In the years since Goering had gone into exile, his old enemy Alfred Rosenberg had risen in the party ranks, and he had none but unkind words for the former No. 2 man. He kept reminding Hitler that Goering had been critical of his leadership in the past, and Hitler could not bear any sort of criticism. Further, "Putzi" Hanfstängel, the Munich playboy who had got mixed up with the party, had also risen in influence, largely because of his money. Now he took one look at Goering and saw a paunchy, pale and uncertain figure. He so reported to Hitler with gusto. And so, although Goering had two interviews with the Nazi leader, he was offered nothing in the party.

Once again, Goering turned back the clock to his flying days. He found a job as representative of the Bavaria Motor Works (BMW), which was just then trying to get into the airplane-engine business, and he went to Berlin to try to sell aircraft engines. There he encountered several of his old flying friends, including his first air commander, Bruno Loerzer, who was now associated with the new airline Lufthansa. They talked of the old days and of the stirrings of military aviation in the new Germany. Ernst Udet had gone into commercial flying and then into the aircraft construction business, which he promoted by air racing. The firms of Dornier, Heinkel, Junkers, and Rohrbach were also competing in this brisk business. Germany was forbidden, of course, to have an air force, but there was money to be made abroad—in Argentina and half a dozen other Latin American countries in particular. Then Udet went into the glider business, because, although flying aircraft with engines was sharply restricted in Germany, the sailing of gliders was not. He established a glider factory near Garmisch-Partenkirchen, and by 1927 he had achieved a considerable reputation throughout Germany.

Not Goering. He took a furnished room behind the Kurfürstendamm and began pounding on doors on behalf of BMW. By the end of 1927 he was beginning to make a little headway, and in the spring of 1928 Carin had apparently recovered enough to join him and they moved into a furnished apartment in Berlin, but it was a letdown after the old days of villas and constant entertainment in Munich.

Yet it was only a matter of months before the ebullient Goering had bounced back. He had many contacts, some of them made during the days of von Epenstein's sponsorship, some from the war years, some from the halcyon Munich time before the attempted putsch. He used them all shamelessly and was seen in every popular restaurant and nightclub. Horcher's, the most famous restaurant in Berlin, was his almost daily lunching place.

The word of Goering's success in business and the social milieu reached Hitler down in Munich, and in the spring of 1928 he came up to Berlin and asked Goering to call on him at the little hotel, Sans Souci, where he stayed. Goering appeared, fat and opulent but just as full of Nazi vigor as before and just as eager to rejoin the ranks of the inner brotherhood. Such a course now fitted Hitler's plans. He was planning a serious contest in the coming parliamentary elections, and he needed candidates who were well known and could win. Goering was certainly well known for his war record and, despite his bedraggled appearance in 1927, within the year he had new clothes, an expensive flat and an air of success that meant he was a winner in the business world. He was fat—from this point on he had a constant battle with his weight—but in this period he won some of the skirmishes; when he got too heavy, he would stop eating and go on a furious round of exercise and slimming by sauna and massage.

Goering was just what Hitler needed, once again. He told Hitler he had never lost the Nazi ideals of egalitarianism and loyalty to the common people that the party had professed. Hitler had left those by the wayside in his drive for power for its own sake, but he told Goering that he needed him to help rebuild Germany and that now was the time. And so a new deal was struck, and it was agreed that Goering would lead the candidates of the Nazi party in the coming elections.

CALL TO ARMS

The Fuehrer asked to see his old comrade and welcomed him with open arms, happy to see how well and how prosperous he looked. He asked him to take up the flag again on behalf of the party, and to fight for Germany's redemption at the elections in May.

—Carin Goering in letter to son, Thomas

BLOODY CAMPAIGN

The election campaign was a savage affair. The S.A., emerging refreshed from their brief period of illegality, went to work with gusto, and blood ran in the streets of German cities, greatly to the satisfaction of Goering, who had always favored this type of electioneering.

—Ewan Butler and Gordon Young,
The Life and Death of Hermann Goering

All winter and spring, violence between Communists and Nazis had been increasing, each side sending gangs into the territories of the other. By May the beatings had become killings, and the fever was high as the elections of May 20 approached. Surrounded by Nazi partisans, Goering toured Berlin, making speeches and picking quarrels with his leftist opponents. He did very well as a rough-and-tumble politician, for he had mastered the argot of the Berlin streets and he had sharp sense of humor and ridicule that served very well to put the enemy down.

On May 20, when the votes were counted it became apparent that the Communists and Socialists had won a significant victory, with more than forty percent of the votes. The center had lost ground, but the debacle was reserved for the Nazis: despite all their noise and apparent influence countrywide, they polled only 810,000 votes of a total 31 million cast. They won only a dozen of the 491 seats in the lower house of the Reichstag. The Social Democrats, with 153 seats, were still the most powerful party in Germany, in spite of all Hitler's inveighing against them.

Yet the party's loss was even more Goering's gain, because he won one of those dozen Nazi seats, proving to Hitler that he was indeed a very valuable ally. The other Nazis to go to the Reichstag included Hitler himself and little Dr. Josef Goebbels, the party rabble-rouser.

The victory seemed to give Goering new strength. He had come back to Germany pale and nervous; now he was full of energy, rushing from Reichstag to business meetings. He continued to represent various firms in the aeronautical field and became the lobbyist for the infant airline Lufthansa in the Reichstag. He also was recognized as a valuable party man at this point, and Hitler put him into the speakers' office. So money, which had been very short in the Goering household, suddenly began to come in. He had his eight hundred marks a month as Reichstag deputy, which was a viable middle-class salary. He also had eight hundred marks a month from the Nazi party speakers' bureau for making speeches for the party throughout the country, a thousand marks a month from Lufthansa, and his commissions and expenses from BMW, a Swiss parachute company and several other firms. Suddenly the Goerings were well-to-do. They took a large house on the Badischestrasse, in one of Berlin's better districts, and the entertainment began anew.

But Goering was more than an entertainer. He was respectable, and Hitler recognized that his own need and the party's was for respectability, to win over the German middle class to the Nazi doctrine. Better than anyone else, Goering could present the positive aspects of that doctrine: social democracy for the people, economic democracy for the poor, and curbs on the bankers and industrialists who had sucked the middle class dry in the inflation years (although Hitler put him in charge of propitiating these elements, too). Goering had no personal antipathy to Jews—the head of BMW was an Italian Jew—and where Hitler fulminated, Goering presented reasonable arguments for the Nazi cause. Soon he was making fifteen or twenty speeches a week outside the Reichstag. Through his wife's connections with the Swedish nobility, Goering also moved into circles of the old German nobility, which had been diminished but not killed by the fall of the kaiser.

Even in social matters, Goering showed a shrewdness that was the talk of Berlin. He might call the kaiser's son August Wilhelm "Auwi," but Auwi might find himself at the Goering dinner table sitting next to a motor mechanic from Munich whose entry card was his membership in the Nazi party. The Goering house was open to all. August Wilhelm became a Nazi, and so did his brother Eitel Friedrich. The tycoon Fritz Thyssen came to the Goering house, as did Hjalmar Schacht, the financial wizard. Goering was constantly answering questions and spreading the word of Nazism, and he was at the same time raising money for the party and securing wealthy supporters for Hitler.

In the spring of 1920 Goering was busier than ever. Meetings, speeches, long trips to the far reaches of Germany to lure new supporters were the order of every week. Carin fell ill again: the pace was far too fast for her, and she was in and out of hospital, bed and sanatorium. Goering never faltered.

Egged on by Dr. Goebbels' propaganda machinery in Berlin and the *Völkischer Beobachter,* the Nazis in Berlin grew bold and engaged in frequent street battles with the Communists and Socialists. In one such battle, a Nazi bullyboy named Horst Wessel was killed, and Goebbels pulled out all the party publicity machinery to make a martyr of the man. Martyrdom demanded a considerable effort in tidying up Wessel's unsavory gangster past, but Goebbels was up to the job, and it was not long before the ladies and gentlemen who gathered at the Goering table were singing the praises of a man they had never known.

During this spring of 1930, the Nazi party faced a serious crisis of identity. Goering was making fine inroads into the capitalist class, Goebbels was appealing to the workers and middle-class Germans, but their efforts were being undermined by the behavior of the brothers Otto and Gregor Strasser, who hailed back to the original tenets of the party, the radicalism of the past when the Nazis had sneered at parliamentarianism and advocated revolution. Goering complained that the Strassers undermined him; he would be working on some big industrialist for a financial contribution, and the Strassers would then stage a raid on the industrialist's factory.

The Strassers had taken over an element of the SA, and in the spring Hitler saw them as a major threat to his leadership of the party. He called the brothers to a meeting, and the result was the capitulation of Gregor Strasser to Hitler, and the walkout of Otto Strasser, who formed his own splinter revolutionary group.

At almost the same time began another rebellious movement within the SA, whose members had become very full of themselves. They demanded a raise in pay, and when they did not get it, they came to Berlin, entered the party offices where Dr. Goebbels held forth, and ransacked them. All of this was a part of the spasm in which the growing Nazi party found itself, with enormous growth in such a hurry. It was also a preface to the Nazi Party Congress of 1930 in Nuremberg, the largest rally so far and an event that so established Nuremberg as the home of the party that in future all rallies would be held there. The storm troopers were very much in evidence—a band now grown to number 100,000 men, and one about which Hitler had some serious misgivings.

In the early days, Goering had loved his role as head of the SA. It had appealed to the swashbuckling side of his nature. Now he wanted the leadership back, but Hitler was shrewd enough to know that he must not invest too much power in one person, so the Nazi leader ignored Goering's yearnings and turned instead to Ernst Röhm, the former army officer who had been Goering's deputy. Röhm had sickened of the rigors of German life and had gone off to South America to train soldiers for the Bolivian army. SA Commander Pfeffer von Salomon was promoted to a vague job in Munich, and Röhm was offered the command. He accepted swiftly. Goering was disappointed but he concealed it, and Hitler rewarded him with a new title of "chief political representative."

As these problems were being sorted out, on 14 September 1930 Germans again went to the polls to elect a national legislature. This time the Nazis polled 6.5 million votes and sent 107 representatives to the lower house of the Reichstag, to become the second largest party in the German Parliament. The Social Democrats still had the most seats (142), but they were failing fast in the wake of the worldwide depression that had begun in the winter of 1929–30. The Nazi problem was that the Communists were the third most powerful party in Germany, with more than four million votes, and they promised in their own way to better the lot of the German people. Hitler had to persuade the people that he could do so more effectively.

One area in which the Nazis grew active was the army, which was afraid of the Nazis because of the brownshirts (SA) and blackshirts (SS), which were military organizations. But Hitler denied that they were really military in nature, and said the army had nothing to fear from the Nazis. The generals were not easily convinced. So the Nazis turned to the young officers and began spreading their propaganda. Three young officers were caught in the act, charged and sent to court-martial for violating their trust. Two actually went to trial. When the case was tried, at Leipzig, Hitler appeared as a witness and made a point of assuring the generals that the Nazis would not interfere with the army.

Largely because of his speech, the defendants were convicted—a matter that should have been a warning to all who associated with Hitler that they were likely to be thrown to the wolves if such a move would help him.

In his days as a salesman Goering had begun to meet influential German businessmen and lure them into the party

HITLER THE POLITICIAN

Evading all attempts to make him sound like the rabble-rousing leader of a military and rebellious force, he used every opportunity to emphasize that his party was seeking power not through violence but through the ballot box, and that the "enemies of Germany will be crushed by us legally," as would "the iniquities of the Treaty of Versailles."

"Another two or three elections, and we will have the majority in the Reichstag," he said at trial in Leipzig. "Then power will be ours and a people's tribunal will judge the November criminals. And I frankly predict that then you will see heads rolling in the sand."

or at least into support of the party. He introduced Hitler to many of them, and by the winter of 1930 they were pleased to meet the rising star of German politics. They included Georg von Schnitzler of I. G. Farben, the chemical trust; August Rosterg and August Diehn of the potash industry; Otto Wolf, the Cologne industrial magnate; and Baron Kurt von Schröder, the Cologne banker. These were names of power and importance in Germany in 1930, and even a year earlier they would have paid no attention to Adolf Hitler, but times had changed and Hitler was putting on his best face, that of parliamentary statesman, and he would deny all the claims of the past that he was willing to overthrow the democratic processes in favor of his own revolution.

Nineteen thirty-one opened with the world still suffering from depression. Hitler had added to Ernst Röhm's control of the storm troopers overall command of the Schutzstaffel

(SS), the black-shirted personal bodyguard of Adolf Hitler, which was commanded directly by Heinrich Himmler, a pinch-faced little man in a pince-nez, who had been trained as a farmer.

The Nazi party was now the strongest in Germany, and everyone knew it when they walked out of the Reichstag in an argument and virtually paralyzed the government. But in October Hitler called the Nazis back to Berlin, and they appeared once more in the Reichstag.

Hermann Goering was now once again definitely ensconced as the No. 2 man of the Nazi party. When Hitler engineered a meeting with President von Hindenburg, a part of his plan to take over the government through parliamentary means, Goering was by his side. And when von Hindenburg, having got to know Hitler, revealed himself contemptuous of the Nazis, Goering and Hitler conferred and agreed that it would be better to continue with the democratic processes than to put the SA and the SS on the streets to stage a revolution, as they had at the beer hall in Munich.

But to use the parliamentary procedure they still needed a crisis. That crisis was provoked by Ernst Röhm's brownshirts, who now numbered more than 400,000 men. The Communists and the Socialists had their own private armies, and these groups clashed ever more frequently as Röhm put on the pressure.

Elections were scheduled for 31 July 1932. June was marked by scores of confrontations in the streets of many cities. On July 17, when the Nazis staged a march through the working-class district of Hamburg, it was a pure provocation of the Communists, and they replied with an attack. In the street fighting which followed, nineteen people were killed and nearly three hundred injured.

The Nazis redoubled their efforts, the brownshirts guarding Nazi rallies and invading the Communists' rallies. Goering spoke in Munich to more than 40,000 people. Hitler had an audience of 225,000 on July 27 in Berlin.

When the votes were counted, the Nazis had become the largest party in the Reichstag, with 230 seats, the Social Democrats diminished to 133. Even if the Communists and Socialists combined, the Nazis still had more seats, so although they did not have a clear majority, they had the strongest working force. Goering began planning for a Nazi takeover. He went to Munich and conferred with party leaders, and with leaders of other parties. He schemed to force von Hindenburg to appoint Hitler as chancellor. Von Hindenburg, despising Hitler, resisted. He showed this at an icy meeting with Hitler in August, at which time he turned down Hitler's request to be made chancellor.

BLIND TO THE DANGER

Make that man my chancellor? I'll make him a postmaster, and he can lick stamps with my head on them!
—Von Hindenburg

After that Hitler and Goering and the other party faithful conferred. Röhm wanted to send the storm troopers into the streets to seize power. Goering persuaded Hitler to use only political process.

As a result of the elections of 1932 and the Nazi surge, Goering was the head of the Nazi parliamentary group, and he was also elected president of the Assembly, the lower house, which made him the most powerful member of that body. As such he used his power and influence to try to lessen the distrust of President von Hindenburg (whom Goering admired) for Adolf Hitler. The problem was Franz von Papen, a von Hindenburg favorite, who had no political power of his own but the hand of the president on his shoulder. Von Papen was the chancellor designate, but he had no real base.

In September 1932, von Papen made a bid for absolute control. He persuaded von Hindenburg to give him the power to dissolve the Reich whenever he felt it necessary. His plan was to create confusion in the house by attacking the Communists, and then to dissolve the legislature. But Goering heard about it and conspired with the Communists. They offered a vote of censure of the chancellor. The Nazis were supposed to rise up against this because of their dislike of the Communists, but they followed Goering's orders and agreed. Von Papen came up to the podium with his order of dissolution of the house, but the house had just voted by 513 to 32 to censure the chancellor, which meant no confidence and removal from office. Goering read the vote first, and then the order to dissolve, and noted that it had been offered to the house by a chancellor who had just been removed from office.

And so there were elections once again in December 1932. The Nazis lost some ground, but Goering was again elected president of the Reichstag. In this capacity he bribed, rigged, arranged, fiddled and persuaded until he had secured the support of the generals and of enough politicians to put Hitler in power. On 29 January 1933 von Hindenburg agreed to Goering's request that he appoint Hitler chancellor, as the only man capable of bringing Germany out of its difficulties.

Dr. Goebbels said it was Goering's finest hour. Everyone in the know agreed that the appointment had been engineered by Goering, and even Hitler was grateful. Goering became minister without portfolio in the cabinet, and also minister of the interior of Prussia; Wilhelm Frick became minister of the interior of the federal government, but all the other jobs were given to non-Nazis by President von Hindenburg's demand. He wanted to keep a sharp eye on Hitler. His principal instrument was still Franz von Papen, whom Hitler had been forced to accept as vice-chancellor. Any time Hitler wanted to see von Hindenburg, he was supposed to bring von Papen with him, a bitter pill.

And so Hitler had power. It was 30 January 1933, and the event was celebrated by a huge torchlight parade past the Chancellery, where Hitler stood at a window giving the Nazi salute, while Goering, behind him, broadcast the proceedings to the nation.

Then the Nazis settled down to make their plans for seizure of *total* power.

As Prussian minister of the interior, Goering was in charge of the Berlin police. He began searching the dossiers of all the important politicians to discover who were the anti-Nazis. They would be dealt with first. And they were. One by one they received notices of retirement or dismissal, and Nazis were put in their places. The SA and the SS were made auxiliaries of the police. Dr. Goebbels was appointed minister of propaganda and thus gained control of press and radio. In a month Goebbels had taken control of the whole mechanism of public safety in the central core of Germany.

At that point Hitler was ready to act. His appointment from von Hindenburg had been hedged with a proviso that, if there was dissension within the cabinet, the government would be dissolved and a new election held. Once the groundwork for seizure of power was accomplished, Hitler

TRIUMPHANT ADDRESS

My German comrades, as I stand here at the microphone, hundreds of thousands of our people are massed outside the Reich Chancellery. They are in a mood which can only be compared with the enthusiasm of August 1914, when the nation stood up to defend Fatherland, honor and freedom. January 30, 1933, will enter Germany's history as the day on which the nation, after fourteen years of anguish, pain, and shame, is restored to its former glory— see the great field marshal who has united himself now with the young generation. He stands beside the young new Fuehrer who will lead the nation to a new and better future. May the German people herald this day as it is acclaimed by the hundreds of thousands in front of these windows, inspired by the new faith [that] the future will bring us what we have fought for in spite of reverses and disappointments: Bread and work for the German people, freedom and honor for the nation.

—Goering on radio broadcast

and Goering conferred, and Hitler created a crisis over an obscure issue, announced that to govern in such circumstances was impossible and called for new elections. They were to be held on 5 March 1933.

Goering held a big party at his official mansion, and Hitler invited all the important magnates of business and finance. Dr. Hjalmar Schacht passed the hat for donations to the party coffers and collected three million marks in half an hour. The party was well enough heeled now to do almost anything legal.

And extralegal. Goering staged a raid on the Communist party headquarters and claimed to have found documents proving that the Communists were preparing to burn down many public buildings, including the Reichstag, in staging a revolution.

On the night of February 27 someone did burn down the Reichstag. Later, many were to say that Goering had done it himself, but that seems most unlikely. No evidence was ever found to indicate his hand in the affair—even in the Nuremberg-trial days, when all Nazi records were open. He always claimed that he needed no such provocation to move against the Communists, because he had all sorts of evidence of their conspiracies to seize power.

GOERING'S VENDETTA

The record of Communists crimes was already so long and their offense so atrocious that I was in any case resolved to use all the powers at my disposal in order ruthlessly to wipe out this plague.

—Goering

The burning of the Reichstag filled Hitler with delight. He expected an outright majority in the coming elections. He did not get it. The Nazis polled forty-four percent of the vote, which was the best any party had done for years, but they did not get a majority. Absolute power would have to come in another manner. Goering found it. On 23 March 1934 he ordered the arrest of all the Communist deputies on charges of conspiracy to overthrow the government by force and violence; and with the Communist deputies absent the Nazis could muster two-thirds of the votes of the house and pass an act enabling Hitler to govern by decree. Hitler became the dictator of Germany, and Goering was at his right hand.

6

POWER PLAY

The period after the Reichstag fire was named by Hitler *Machtbefestung*—the consolidation of power. It was in this period that Goering also consolidated his place with Hitler.

Following their reconciliation, on his return from Sweden, Goering's value to Hitler had been his skill as a "meeter and greeter" and as a political leader. He had become, of course, a leading parliamentary figure, but to the Nazis that was nothing, because they had no intention of maintaining a parliamentary system. However, during the period of cementing power, they had to work through the system, and Goering led the struggle.

Yet he was the first to recognize the temporary nature of his power, and he set about finding a new base. That is why he wormed out of Franz von Papen, chief of the Prussian cabinet, the post of Prussian minister of the interior. It was apparently not nearly so important a job as his post of speaker of the Reichstag, or that of minister without portfolio in Hitler's federal cabinet, but appearances were deceiving. Hitler approved because this appointment gave the Nazis a road into the politics of Prussia, and Prussia held a

special place in the German scheme of things as the organizing power of a limited Germany.

The immediate effect of the appointment was to make
Goering head of the Prussian police, with access to police
dossiers on thousands of political figures. He knew precisely
how he wanted to use this power. On his first day as minister,
he began campaigns of harassment against the rival parties,
particularly the Communists and the Social Democrats. The
Communists had a permit to hold a demonstration that day.
Goering canceled it. The Social Democrat newspaper complained about Goering's high-handedness. He suspended
publication for three days.

Goering sensed the power of his position from the beginning and used it to eliminate the strength of the Socialists
and the Communists, the principal competitors of the Nazis.
As noted elsewhere, he also began the purging of officials. In
this activity, his conservative, upper-middle-class background played an important role. He had the confidence in
the beginning of the conservative officials of old Prussia who
had looked askance at the coming of the Social Democrats
under the Weimar Republic. One of these, Rudolf Diels,
became a willing conspirator, in the belief that the purge of
the Socialists would strengthen the conservatives in Prussia.
But Diels soon found that he was riding a tiger. Goering was
ruthless in eliminating anyone who got in his way, and soon
a whole group of conservative officials also felt the boot.

To accomplish all this quickly Goering needed allies, and
he found them in the ranks of the SA, his old organization,
and the SS. He awarded appointments as auxiliary police,
which gave them the legal right to continue their bullyboy
tactics.

After the Reichstag fire, Goering led the fight that quickly disposed of the Communists, in his heartfelt belief that they were preparing a revolution to take over Prussia.

With a great deal of help from Goering in his new job, as well as through his efforts in Parliament itself and as a speaker on the streets, the Nazis won a big victory in the elections of March 5. Hitler still had to tread slowly, but Goering brought ever more Nazis into positions of authority in Prussia, and every little bit helped.

By April the Nazis had so consolidated their power that Goering was moved to a new post, as deputy to Hitler.

GLORY AT LAST

At last Goering could afford to relax. . . . Now he reigned, after Hitler, supreme in Germany, and none would dare again to challenge him.

—Ewan Butler and Gordon Young,
The Life and Death of Hermann Goering

A few weeks before Hitler's assumption of dictatorial powers, Hermann Goering had predicted enormous change to the nation in a radio broadcast: "We are now closing the darkest era of German history and are beginning a new chapter."

The visible hallmark was terror.

Goering set up his own police force, the Geheime Staatspolizei, who would gain so formidable a reputation under their short title "Gestapo." So many people were being arrested on so many charges that something had to be done to accommodate the prisoners. As head of the police, Goering was responsible for the establishment of concentration camps. There came the thousands of Germans arrested for being Communists, Catholics, Jews or free thinkers. Hundreds of people were herded into the new camps. The Nazis had their revenge on all who had opposed them, and the storm troopers began to set up their own camps, where acts of great brutality were carried out. One day when a friend of Goering's mistress, Emmy Sonnemann, was arrested and Goering intervened to get him out, it was a great embarrassment to discover that the man had already suffered a broken arm and a broken jaw at the hands of the SA.

Goering attempted to intercede and keep the camps as internment camps rather than brutality centers, but he was not very successful. Particularly Heinrich Himmler, the head of the SS, managed several horror camps, one at Osnabrück and another at Dachau, from which the most dreadful rumors escaped, tales of murder and torture that some found hard to believe.

Goering also used the SA to cleanse all the government offices of people inimical to the Nazis. In doing this, however, he made many enemies in the lower ranks of the party and among the people who wanted to get close to Hitler, and so he began to restrain the power he had given the SA. But the problem was that the SA had, in a way, passed beyond his personal control and, even more important in the shaping of Germany in the next few months, it had given some ideas to Ernst Röhm, who had taken over the national SA from Goering and was now getting some tips on how to use its power to the greatest degree.

Hitler, watching from not far away, took some exception to Goering's use of power and pushed his deputy into yielding some of it over the Gestapo and other police organizations. Goering did not like the change, but he submitted and thus retained position in the first tier of Nazis.

Deprived of some power in Prussia, Goering turned to the national scene again and aligned himself with Goebbels, Robert Ley (a chemist by profession and Nazi party enthusiast) and Heinrich Himmler. He distrusted the latter two men, but he found that Himmler was a better conspirator than he, and made efforts to be agreeable.

7

THE LUFTWAFFE:
IMMACULATE CONCEPTION
OR CONSPIRACY?

Goering ignored the horrors of Nazi social policy. He had many other matters on his mind in the first year of Nazi power, and to him one of the most important was the foundation of a new Luftwaffe.

Nineteen thirty-three was the year in which the German air force again began to come into its own. Goering had never forgotten that day when he had been forced to deliver his precious fighting aircraft into the hands of Germany's enemies. When that first tenuous coalition government had been formed in 1933, Goering had asked Hitler for one extra job and got it. The job was that of minister of aviation.

In the early days no one paid a great deal of attention to the title. It could be seen as the personal aberration of one of Germany's greatest fighter pilots of World War I, fulfillment of an old ambition. There seemed to be scarcely any advantage to the job: it was not even called a ministry but a commission. Under the provisions of the Versailles treaty, Germany had been forbidden the establishment of any air force, so all the commissioner for aviation had to control was the airline Lufthansa and a handful of other flying organizations that were permitted under the law. And the gliders. But as the technology of aviation progressed very rapidly in the 1920s, German businessmen were able to reduce, one by one, the strictures on construction governing size of engines and civil aircraft, until by 1930 the German air industry was able to compete in the world market for airliners and sport planes. Therefore, although there was no visible aviation organization in Germany, there were many trained airmen, waiting in the wings.

The adjutant of the Richthofen fighter squadron was now Colonel Karl Bodenschatz of the German army. Goering sought him out and brought him to his apartment in Berlin for a talk. He reminded Bodenschatz of the old days, when Goering had promised that Germany would once again have a fighting air force. The time had now come, he said, to set the stage for it. Bodenschatz was enthralled, as he always had been with the powerful personality of Hermann Goering. He agreed immediately to transfer from the army to the new air force.

Since Goering did not intend to spend his full time as administrator of the Luftwaffe, his next step was to secure the services of the most knowledgeable air executive in Germany, and perhaps the world. He was Erhard Milch, the chief operator of Lufthansa. But with Milch there were problems. First, he was not a sycophant. He had been a professional officer in the German army, and he regarded Goering as just another fat, sloppy politician. He was not much impressed with Goering's war record or the Pour le Mérite medal. After all, Goering had been Milch's own hireling in his salad days in Berlin when he was seeking desperately for an income, and Milch had given him a thousand marks a month to lobby from inside the Reichstag for Lufthansa. The activity might not have been illegal, but it was certainly not morally strong for a legislator to be a paid lobbyist, too.

Milch's queasiness about working with Goering was soon overcome. Goering could be very persuasive, and he held out a picture of a great military organization to lead all the defense forces of the Third Reich. Milch was convinced when Goering took him to see Hitler, when the chancellor called on Milch's patriotism and told him he must take the job for the sake of Germany.

But there was another problem. Erhard Milch was half Jewish. This was solved by Goering in a circuitous but extremely effective way. He destroyed Milch's heritage and gave him a new one, officially. Milch's father had been a Jew, his mother an Aryan. So Frau Milch was suborned into declaring that her son was the result of a love affair with a German nobleman, and Milch's birth certificate was torn up and a new one issued.

"At least, if we are going to take his real father away from him, let us give him an aristocratic one," said Goering. And thus was Erhard Milch Aryanized.

All this was accomplished in January 1933. Bruno Loerzer was brought in to become head of the Air Sports Club, which was actually the secret training institute for military pilots. Ernst Udet was given a vague post as "adviser" to the air ministry. In fact, he was collecting technicians for the air force.

On 30 January 1933, Hermann Goering appeared at a meeting of the German Aero Club of Berlin. The club was celebrating its twenty-fifth anniversary, and air people from all over Germany had come. Goering brought his staff with him and introduced them. He told the club that big changes were coming. He saw skepticism among the audience, so long battered down by the enforcers of the Versailles treaty. So he began listing the changes: subsidies were to be granted immediately for the production of more Junkers 52 planes, more Heinkel 70s, Focke-Wulf 200s and Dornier flying boats. The meeting erupted in cheering, and several men hoisted Goering and carried him around the room.

Soon the money was beginning to flow, and General Werner von Blomberg, the war minister, transferred some of his most aggressive younger officers to the Luftwaffe, recognizing the need for the attack philosophy there.

So sub rosa, the German air force was being re-created in 1933. Actually the spirit of German aviation had never died out, although it had been so seriously restricted since the end of World War I, for German air enthusiasts had kept the aviation tradition alive despite the Versailles treaty's attempt to destroy it. The Junkers firm built a factory for the Soviet Union and one at Malmö in Sweden, to augment several factories in Germany where parts were made. There was nothing in the Versailles treaty to outlaw the manufacture of airplane parts, just airplanes. So the aircraft were assembled elsewhere. The Versailles treaty also explains why the Germans developed trimotor aircraft instead of twin-engine: because they were constrained to build aircraft engines of only a certain size. Thus came the Fokker trimotor, one of the most advanced airliners of the period between the wars.

There were other ways of beating the rules imposed by the victors. Dr. Claudius Dornier set up a factory at Altentheim, on Lake Constance, which was just a few miles from his old factory at Friedrichshafen. And even as the Allies policed the German air, Dornier was perfecting the flying boat on neutral soil. Northwest of Frankfurt am Main, in the Rhône Mountains, young men were learning how to glide.

Ernst Udet had gone into the aircraft business, as noted, and by the middle of the 1920s had begun producing fast aircraft for racing. At Warnemünde, Ernst Heinkel had produced a low-wing monoplane that was fast and maneuverable. And under Milch's supervision the Germans were really building an air force. One day in 1927 an Englishman who had been a member of the Royal Flying Corps landed at Stettin on a flight across Germany and found there an air training school whose young men wore smart uniforms, clicked their heels, saluted and showed military precision in everything they did. The director of this school volunteered the information that he was training about a hundred pilots a year and that this was only one of six Lufthansa schools. By 1933 Milch had several thousand highly trained officers on his books, no matter what the Versailles treaty said. And all this had been done under the Weimar Republic and Chancellor Heinrich Brüning, long before Hitler came into power.

"Hitler did not start the Luftwaffe. We did," said Chancellor Brüning, interviewed later when he was a refugee in the United States. Brüning had connived with the generals of the small German army to start what they called "the secret air force."

By 1930 a large number of little glider and sport-plane clubs had been amalgamated into the Deutsche Luftfahrt Verband (German League for Aeronautics). In 1934 this organization became the Deutsche Luftsport Verband (German League for Air Sports), which blossomed with uniforms, military precision and a swastika emblem. Through the maintenance of the flying clubs, Germany had thirty first-class airports, and the aircraft being built "for sport" by Willy Messerschmitt and Dr. Heinkel looked more and more like fighters and bombers, while the transport planes looked as though they could easily be converted to heavy bombers. The German aircraft industry was, in fact, at least on a par with that of any other country in the world, a year before the official organization of the Luftwaffe. And it had all been done secretly, so that virtually no one in the world, with the exception of a handful of foreign airmen, had any idea of what was going on.

Writing a history of the Luftwaffe in the 1980s, Williamson Murray said, "Given the fact that no German Air Force survived the Great War, except as a camouflaged planning staff within the army, and that the capacity for civil aircraft production was inadequate for military purposes the development of the *Luftwaffe* was an enormously complex task. . . ." That was true, but to see why it could be accomplished one would have to have gone through the story of German flying and aircraft development in the highly conspiratorial atmosphere of the 1930s, when Erhard Milch was planning, planning, planning. The development of the Luftwaffe in the middle 1930s was not as difficult as it appeared. The groundwork had been well done.

Hermann Goering started it all very quietly. In 1934 the appropriation for the air ministry was seventy-eight million marks, and the Luftwaffe was only one of six departments, even its name camouflaged as "air protection" and its place in the scheme lying between the section of the ministry devoted to sporting aviation and that devoted to press and information. A year later the ministry's budget was nearly four times as large. And that year Erhard Milch, the secretary of state for air, was commissioned a general. Milch and the Nazis' predecessors had planned very thoroughly in every direction. A new air-ministry building had already been designed and was immediately put under construction.

C. C. Grey, one of Britain's leading airmen, visited the Air Ministry soon after it opened: ". . . one of the most impressive buildings I have ever seen," he said. "On the first story on one side is a huge conference room capable, I should think, of seating five hundred people, and on the other side is a hall for official receptions which combines unusual beauty of proportion and decoration with the most modern lighting tricks. The whole atmosphere of the room can be changed according to which set of lights are turned on and it gives something of the feeling of awe which one has in a cathedral. . . ." That was no accident. Hermann Goering was very much the showman. He knew the value of impressing those around him. And he knew what he wanted and where he intended to go.

Before the building was finished, the Berlin correspondent of one London newspaper jeered that the ministry was going to have a thousand rooms.

"What will they do with them?" he asked.

He would find out soon enough. Actually there were 1,500 rooms, and Goering was soon complaining that they were not enough.

In 1935 the Luftwaffe was formally organized, flouting the Versailles treaty. By that time the underground organization had provided 900 flying officers, 200 antiaircraft officers and 17,000 enlisted men. The idea then was to expand it by 1939 to 15,000 officers and 370,000 men.

Major General Christiansen was put in charge of training, which had eight divisions, ranging from physical training schools to a staff college. Ernst Udet had been brought back into the service as a colonel to take charge of the technical departments. The Luftwaffe had its own signals organization and its own antiaircraft artillery. Its first air squadron, naturally named the Richthofen Geschwader (Richthofen Wing), was formed in 1935. It consisted of one *Geschwader* (wing), commanded by a colonel; three *Gruppen* (groups), each commanded by a major, made up a *Geschwader*. A *Gruppe* consisted of three *Staffel* (squadrons), each commanded by a captain. A *Staffel* consisted of three *Ketten* (flights), each commanded by a lieutenant. The *Kette* was the lowest operating unit.

From the beginning, Goering insisted that his people have the best. A British observer invited to visit the air staff college at Gatow-Kladow was escorted into a big messroom with an attractive bar, a reading room and a silent room for writing. He said he was pleased to see that the officers had so much comfort.

"This is not the officers' mess," said his escort. "This is the transport drivers' mess."

And the British visitor was then taken to the officers' mess, which reminded him of Claridge's Hotel in London.

In the beginning, General Milch offered Goering a study that suggested the building of a fleet of four hundred heavy bombers, which could deliver a strategic bombing campaign anywhere in Europe. Had it been built, the Battle of Britain might have taken another turn, but it was not then built, because the German army objected to the concept of air superiority above all else, and because the German aircraft industry lacked experience in the building of such large craft and such designers as Fokker and Heinkel were not then interested. The project limped along in 1934 and 1935 but was canceled in 1936 when it became apparent that the German aircraft industry was not producing engines strong enough for the task.

In 1933 Germany produced a thousand planes for the secret Luftwaffe. General Milch was organizing the work force: as promised by Goering, he could have his pick of the six million German unemployed.

When Goering took office as air minister in 1933, the German concept of air power was that it should be an adjunct to land and sea forces, a concept quite general throughout the world. However, by 1934 a new concept had captured the leaders of the Luftwaffe. The air force would both support the army and the navy and be prepared to carry air attack to the enemy and to defend Germany's airspace. It was a tall order. A key element, according to Milch, was that "the terrorizing of the enemy's chief cities and industrial regions through bombing, would lead that much more quickly to a collapse of morale; weaken the national character of his people, and social and political rifts will cleave his society." So bombing was to be a psychological as well as physical weapon for the Germans.

Like the British, Goering saw the air force as a separate institution and, like many air leaders worldwide, believed in the power of an air force to decide a war. Therefore from the beginning he began working to remove the army air force from army control and the naval air forces from naval control. Until 1933 the Air Office of the defense ministry had managed all air affairs on land. That office had undertaken the building of a secret Luftwaffe. Within a year Goering had secured complete control of air policy and procurement for the Luftwaffe, and by 1936 the Luftwaffe was accepted as a separate military organization, equal to the army and navy.

As head of the Luftwaffe, Goering has been faulted for appointing Milch, for politicizing the air force, for employing many army officers to establish the air force and for appointing friends and contacts. This, it seems to this writer, is somewhat farfetched. Goering had to have a manager, and Milch was the best in a number of countries. He had to have trained officers who could impose discipline on the infant air force, and the army could supply those admirably. The skills of flight and flight management are quite apart from the military skills of leadership. As for appointment of friends, many of those friends had gained experience in the World War I German flying service, and others were professional contacts Goering had made along the way. Whether they were cronies or Nazis, the important matter ought have been whether or not they could perform adequately in their jobs. Some, such as Ernst Udet, started out brilliantly (in Stuka dive-bombers) but fell along the way.

The basic problems of the German air force in World War II were created in the 1930s, when army and navy collaborated to complain about Luftwaffe budgets and thus to prevent the development of a heavy-bomber command, and also by the failure to develop second- and third-generation fighter planes, which the Western Allies were doing.

8

WHICH PLACE FOR GOERING?

Nineteen thirty-four was a year of change for the Nazis. Ernst Röhm, who had been Goering's competitor for control of the SA, gained that control when Goering took on a number of other jobs, including that of formulating the economy of the Third Reich. But Röhm was overreaching himself, and through his own police force Goering found out how greatly. Röhm revealed the extent of his ambitions one day in February 1934, when he proposed to a cabinet meeting that the SA, the SS and the army be merged into a superarmy, with himself as minister of defense. The army took violent exception to the plan, and Goering saw where it was leading. Soon General von Blomberg was seeking an audience with Hitler to tell him what the army thought of the idea. Hitler, too, said he was shocked and told von Blomberg that the SA was never going to take over anything. He would see that Röhm's ambitions were calmed down.

Hitler and Röhm had a confrontation, at which Röhm accused Hitler of betraying the revolution planned by the National Socialists and selling out to the army.

Goering knew then that Röhm must be eliminated, for

in the confrontation Röhm had let his hatred of Goering show, accusing him of wanting only to feather his own nest. Through Goering's police, he kept tabs on the telephone conversations of the SA leaders. His ears must have burned, for Röhm and his friends spoke of Goering as "that fat pig" and discussed what they would do when they killed him.

THE HATE OF HIS ENEMIES

I will personally slice slabs of flesh off his fat body, until he is half his size, and only then will I stick my knife in his throat.

—Karl Ernst about Goering

Do that, but don't eat any of the cuts. Forbidden meat!

—Ernst Röhm about Goering

At the end of the first week of June 1934, Röhm left Berlin for a sanatorium at Wiessee, a lake in upper Bavaria. His principal aide, Karl Ernst, stayed in Berlin, although he had just got married. No one gave any sign of the bitter struggle that was raging within the party for control.

Röhm and Ernst were in constant telephone communication, and Goering's police were listening in. Checking around, Goering discovered that, although Röhm was "on holiday," his SA men were prepared for action. All this was passed to Hitler, and on June 25 he put the military forces of the government on a state of alert, expecting some action from the SA to seize power.

Rudolf Hess made a speech at Cologne, egged on by Hitler, at which he called on all elements in the party to unite and not to try to stage a second revolution. But Röhm, although hearing, was not listening. He called a meeting of his SA executives at his sanatorium for June 30.

Hitler was very nervous, apparently afraid of the disruption Röhm might cause. Goering was determined: Röhm had gone too far and must be eliminated. Before the end of June he had all his police alerted and was prepared for civil war.

Karl Ernst felt that Goering was up to something and telephoned him, but Goering was all smiles and sweetness and reminded Ernst that he had attended the wedding. Why not go off and take a nice honeymoon, he suggested.

So Ernst telephoned Röhm and said all was well. The "leadership" conference was scheduled to go on, and Hitler announced that he would make an appearance.

It was quite true; he did make an appearance. Shortly after midnight on 30 June 1934, he set out in a car with a gang of Nazi killers. Before dawn they reached the sanatorium, and one by one they murdered the SA leaders. One, who seemed to offer Hitler resistance, was beaten before he was killed. Röhm was offered a chance to commit suicide, refused and was shot.

Meanwhile, in Berlin, Goering and his police had surrounded the brownshirt headquarters. Goering had a list of the dangerous ones, and he consulted it as he went from room to room.

On the road to Bremen, Karl Ernst was tracked down, torn from the arms of his bride and brought back to Berlin, where he was put up against a wall and shot by an SS firing squad. He was not alone: by the score, the SA men designated by Goering were brought to the firing wall, and there they were shot down in groups of half a dozen. Other brown-shirts were rounded up and taken to Goering's house, where he consulted his list and decided whether they should live or die. He saved the life of Franz von Papen that night, though von Papen had been designated by Himmler to die and Hitler had agreed. Goering kept von Papen at his own house all night and early in the morning sent him home under house arrest, protected by Goering's police from Himmler's SS.

The slaughter continued until Goering brought an end to it on the second day, when he observed that Himmler and his assistant, Reinhardt Heydrich, were using Hitler's fury and fears as grounds to carry out their own vendettas against their old enemies. Goering saw that this could create many problems for himself and for Hitler.

The bloodshed stopped. About 150 people, all of them of some political significance in the Third Reich, had fallen beneath the hands of the party rulers.

THE IRON FIST

The Fuehrer told the Reichstag two weeks after the "re-volt" was put down: "Meanwhile Minister President Goering had previously received my instructions that in case of a purge, he was to take analogous measures at once in Berlin and in Prussia. With an iron fist he beat down the attack on the National Socialist state before it could develop."

So Berlin quieted down. President von Hindenburg, when told the Goering side of the story, approved heartily of the stamping-out of what he saw as high treason.

WITHOUT MERCY

When circumstances require it, one must not shrink from the most extreme action. One must be able to spill blood also.

—Von Hindenburg to Hitler

And the party seemed to grow stronger with the elimination of the radical wing.

PRAISING THE PURGE

They [the president, the minister of justice, and the generals] in fact despised that eruption of plebeian hatred. Their open display of sympathy for Hitler's intervention sprang from quite different causes: in the Blood Purge of June 30, 1934, the strong left wing of the party, represented chiefly by the SA, was eliminated.

—Albert Speer

The SA once again looked to Goering. His position as the second man in the Third Reich was at this point unassailable.

President von Hindenburg died early in August, and on his death Hitler decided there was nothing to be gained by prolonging the charade of democratic regime. He announced that, as of this moment, the office of president of the Third Reich would be combined with that of chancellor and that he, Hitler, would become head of state as well as commander of the armed forces, and director of the body politic.

Hermann Goering put on the dress uniform of general of

the Luftwaffe that he had designed for himself, and assembled the senior officers of his new Luftwaffe at the Air Ministry. He told them of von Hindenburg's death, and his voice broke. But that was not all. He called on his officers to swear an oath of allegiance to Adolf Hitler, and they did. They were the first military body to do so and thus won for themselves a firm place in the heart of the German dictator. Goering's loyalty to Hitler was incontrovertible, and at this point it entered his new military organization. Almost immediately the new position of the Luftwaffe would become apparent in the military budget of the Third Reich.

In spite of Hermann Goering's apparent rank in the Nazi Party in 1934, after the elimination of Ernst Röhm, he still felt like an outsider. He had sacrificed a great deal in those years 1923–31 when he was a fugitive from Germany, and his cool reception by the Führer on his return had been a shock. He had carried out the purge of the SA in Prussia, as Himmler had in Bavaria, but while Goering's actions were highly applauded (winning a special message from President von Hindenburg, for example), he still did not feel secure.

In the autumn of 1934 Goering's position depended on his command of the Luftwaffe, in which he was subordinate to General von Blomberg, the army chief of staff, and on his personal relations with Hitler, to whom he was a sounding board. He would have liked to try his hand at foreign affairs, but von Neurath, the foreign minister, was extremely jealous of his prerogatives and recognized in Goering a real threat, for he could see that Goering was both extremely curious and ambitious and that he was looking for a secure niche for himself.

Goering did manage to creep around the edges of foreign-policy determination, because of his intimacy with Hitler and

because of Hitler's misapprehension that Goering had gar-
nered special knowledge and special credentials in southern
European affairs during his stay in the south when he was a
fugitive. Hitler did not realize that this was all a front, that
Mussolini regarded Goering as a self-serving fool, "a former
inmate of a lunatic asylum."

However, Goering did have certain influence in long-range
matters. He convinced Hitler that Germany should tie itself
closely to Japan, as the future leader in Asia, although most
German diplomacy had favored China since the old days of
Germany's Kiaochao colony in Shantung province. Thus
Goering had a certain responsibility for setting up the conditions of the Rome–Berlin–Tokyo axis. Also, as anyone who
visited China would observe, he managed to persuade the
Nationalist government into buying thousands of unwieldy
Mauser machine pistols of the 1920s, and thus Chinese policemen in their yellowish uniforms could be seen everywhere
with these enormous weapons at their belts. In this aspect
Goering was his old self, the arms salesman, and he reaped
a nice commission on the sale.

Nevertheless, except for his special missions on behalf of
the Führer, Goering was kept out of the foreign-affairs arena
by the diplomatic corps, who resented his intrusions.

In assessing Goering, one must remember that he was the
most loyal to Hitler of all the people around the Führer in
this period, and because Hitler recognized this doglike devo-
tion, Goering came to occupy a special place in the Nazi
hierarchy that had nothing to do with any of his many titles.

Between 1934 and 1936, when Goering was devoting most
of his attention to the building of the Luftwaffe, he also
undertook a number of special duties for the Führer but had
no major role in German government. Though the impor-

tance of the Prussian ministry declined as the Nazis took control of the whole state, Goering did not need that crutch any longer—although, typically, as his power over the local SA and Gestapo and ordinary police was removed, with Hitler's assent, he struggled all the way.

This was the period in which he established his special role as the chief showman of the Third Reich. He loved luxury, of course, and his house in Berlin was modern in architectural design and a compendium of the finest in furnishings, crystal and everything else that money could buy. He designed his own flamboyant Luftwaffe uniforms, favoring the blue and white, and those of his officers and men as well. One reason for the flamboyance was his natural vulgarity, but another was deadly serious: to make the Luftwaffe so outstanding in every way that it would impress the world.

Since Hitler was not at ease with strangers and had virtually no small talk at his disposal, Goering became his chief entertainer. This had been true, of course, in the very earliest days, when his house in Munich had been the social headquarters of the Nazi party, where Hitler and the rest used to gather in the evenings and drink beer and plot their future. Now, with the trappings of chief deputy, Goering stepped out and entertained the lords of German industry and the leaders of European political society. He did a good job: almost everyone who came into contact with him gained a good impression of the Nazi hierarchy, although it might well be changed by encounters with other members or a view of life in the real, anti-Semitic police state that Germany had already become.

In 1936 Goering found a new niche for himself in the running of the Third Reich. He became Germany's business manager.

Those who saw Goering as the smiling pilot and those who

saw him as the fat buffoon were surprised, but the fact was that he had the ability and the contacts for this job. When he had first come to Berlin and been elected to the Reichstag, he had made a name for himself in economic affairs.

Goering came to Hitler's attention in this regard because he supported Hitler's view that Germany must undertake a vast program of armament. In 1934 he introduced a bill into the cabinet calling for the control of all armament factories by the state. He also suggested that Germany build and operate her own raw-material plants to be sure of materials for armament. At the time those ideas did not succeed, largely because of the opposition of the German army, but Hitler did not forget them. After 1934, although the army objected to the use of so much of Germany's resources by the Luftwaffe, Goering and Milch insisted that the air army be built up as rapidly as possible, and they found Hitler's ear, because Goering suggested that, if the air army was strong enough, Hitler could win concessions politically from other countries without warfare. So the air strength was doubled in 1934, and Goering asked again for its doubling in 1935.

In 1935 Goering also proved his ability and his independence in economic thinking. The issue was a quarrel between Hjalmar Schacht, minister for economics, and Agricultural Minister Walther Darré over a food shortage that threatened stability in Germany. Schacht blamed Darré's bad planning, and he was right technically (a poor harvest did not help), but that did not solve the problem. Hitler threw up his hands and asked Goering to handle the matter, and Goering intervened against Schacht, which almost no one else was then willing to do, and sided with Darré in favor of more money for food imports. Since Goering's demands for money for the Luftwaffe had been one of the factors in causing the shortage of foreign exchange, this was a brave move, and Hitler was impressed.

Hjalmar Schacht was the leader of the conservative element in the Third Reich, which hoped to propitiate the Nazis or to woo them from their radical ideas. Schacht in particular felt he could manage Goering, whom he saw as a babe in the economic woods. And so Schacht was responsible for the promotion of Goering in the Reich's economic planning. In 1936, he suggested that Hitler give Goering an important job, and Hitler appointed Goering chief of a new Raw Material and Foreign Exchange Office. Hitler was very pleased with the whole idea, because he wanted to bring the economy under party management, which it had not been, and he knew that in Goering he had a totally loyal man who would come to him with all the difficulties. He and Goering also agreed on such matters as synthetic fuels, which would be essential to Germany in case of war and an inability to reach the Middle East's fuel supplies, which dominated the world. The idea was given credulity when Romania, then Europe's principal source of petroleum, threatened to cut off Germany's supplies.

In the spring of 1936 Germany reoccupied the Rhineland, and the economic problems appeared more important than ever. Schacht and Darré and others in the economic sphere quarreled about what to do, and finally Hitler appointed Goering—but not just as raw-materials chief. He became a sort of economic controller. When the Spanish civil war broke out in July 1936, Goering was ready: he dispatched a special trade commission to Seville, its major purpose to safeguard the flow of Spanish iron ore to Germany. That year Goering also expropriated all the sources of foreign exchange abroad in the hands of German nationals. This piratical action brought the Third Reich more than a billion marks that year and converted the foreign-exchange deficit into a surplus. He also began the development of synthetic rubber, oil and textiles; he did this initially to save foreign exchange, but in the long term his foresight extended Germany's self-sufficiency and even its ability to prolong the war. As the summer of 1936 drew to a close, Hitler assessed Goering's performance and was pleased. So he decided to put more power into the hands of his deputy.

9

ECONOMIC TSAR

In the summer of 1936 Hitler was planning his war against Europe and possibly the world. In July he drafted a paper which was to be the basis for the Third Reich's Second Four-Year Plan. In August Goering came to Hitler's Bavarian hideaway, and Hitler read the memorandum to him. Then they went for a walk in the grounds, and during that walk Goering was anointed "economic tsar" of Germany in order for him to carry out the Four-Year Plan and prepare the German economy for war.

The news was put out in stages. First, early in September, the Council of Ministers learned that Goering would be the new economic boss of Germany. In the second week of September the party faithful were given a hint of what was to come at the party rally at Nuremberg. Then, secretly, the party leaders were told that this was preparation for war. By the end of October the whole was public knowledge, and Goering was talking about the heavy burden Hitler had given him.

So by the autumn of 1936 Goering truly was the second most important man in all Germany.

From the beginning, Goering had his troubles. The army

did not like the extension of his power, particularly since he was the head of the Luftwaffe, which the generals found an annoyingly competitive organization in terms of its demands for raw materials and financial resources.

Then there were the radical Nazis, the Himmlers and Heydrichs, who had to be watched all the time. Goering had his own way of watching. Years earlier he had established his own intelligence service, whose results he shared only with Hitler. By use of telephone tapping and such tactics, Goering knew pretty well what all his potential rivals were doing all the time.

In December 1936 General von Blomberg forced the issue. At a meeting he presented a paper announcing three army demands about the economy. First that, in case of war, the war ministry should run the economy; second that Hjalmar Schacht's ministry of economics should have the responsibility for running the peacetime economy; and third that Goering should be given responsibility only for raw materials and that if war broke out he would lose even this task to the army.

Hitler read the demands and then ignored them. That was the beginning of the end of von Blomberg.

When Goering took over that year, he announced that the next four years would determine all Germany's economic and social policy. To prepare the people to undergo considerable economic hardship, Dr. Goebbels began a heavy campaign of propaganda, showing that the world had pushed Germany into a corner and that only the heroic activities of the Nazi party could pry the nation out of difficulty.

And so, to prepare for Hitler's war, the government began a planned excursion into deficit spending and into heavy expenditure on armaments.

Germany's businessmen and industrialists predicted economic disaster, but it did not happen. Goering put such tight controls on the civil economy that it *could* not happen. What surprised the military was the ability of the government to persuade the people to buy its bonds: the people did buy them, at levels previously believed impossible. It was an indication of the popularity of the Nazi movement and Nazi policies with the German people. Of course, as Goering admitted, it could be done only in a rigidly controlled state, but he managed to slow up Germany's consumer expenditure by withholding the goods to buy and by increasing taxation, but making these strictures acceptable by promising future prosperity.

Thus the combined efforts of Goebbels and Goering exceeded even the most optimistic hopes of the Führer and confounded the army and the conservative critics of the Nazi regime.

Although Hjalmar Schacht and his associates referred to Goering as "that amateur," in fact he did quite a respectable job, because he knew how to rely on experts while retaining the power of decision.

Goering gained control of the Dresdener Bank and several lesser banks within its orbit, and this gave him power to bypass the Reichsbank, which was controlled by Schacht and his associates, when some issue of note came up.

He also used Nazi go-betweens in the banking business and in the industrial world, to help him work his wonders. I. G. Farben, Germany's largest industrial combine, was brought around to favor the Nazi program of self-sufficiency and war preparation and supported the Four-Year Plan. For their cooperation, I. G. Farben executives gained control over the oil, rubber and explosives industries. Farben had been a very liberal concern, with a number of Jews on its board, but by 1936 all this changed: the board became almost 100 percent Nazi and had close contacts with Goering and his people.

By the end of 1936 Goering was not consulting anyone except Hitler. He was making major decisions that affected every corner of the Third Reich. Theoretically the decisions were controlled by a general council, but in practice the department heads reported directly to Goering, who made the decisions.

All this was accepted reluctantly by the normal governing agencies, as long as the working remained within the purview of the Four-Year Plan, but that did not satisfy Goering. To him, everything in Germany was subject to the Four-Year Plan. The orderly process of budgeting for national expenditures, for example, was usually controlled by the ministry of economics and the ministry of finance, but so pervasive was Goering's activity by the end of 1936 that when General von Blomberg requested an increase in his budget for 1937, he addressed it to Goering. By the end of 1937 Goering had undermined the authority of Economics Minister Hjalmar Schacht.

What Goering was doing was institutionalizing the pledges of National Socialism, a radical philosophy which had promised that the major elements of production would be owned and controlled by the state. Perhaps one of the reasons Hitler so hated Communism was that the net results of Marxist operations were similar to his own. Hitler agreed with Goering that, wherever the interests of private capitalism conflicted with those of the state, the capitalists must go. By 1938 Goering was threatening German capitalism with total state control of the means of production. One of the shorthand definitions of Nazism was that it subjugated and subverted private capitalism yet still retained it, but that was not always true. The Nazis tolerated private capitalism because they needed it; as time went on, their control grew greater and they needed it less. By 1938 Goering controlled more than sixty percent of German industry directly and could change its nature by the stroke of a pen. Consumer industries were decreasing all the time, while heavy industry had more than doubled in the past ten years.

GOERING ON ECONOMICS

I do not acknowledge the holiness of any law about economics. . . . The German economy must always be the servant of the nation.

—Goering

Out of Goering's manipulation, the Third Reich developed some special capabilities. Fritz Todt, later to become the armaments minister, was in charge of construction, and he developed resources and techniques that later enabled him to build mighty fortifications in the military bastions of Hitler's inner empire.

In this period, 1938–39, Goering was in full flower. He was deeply involved in—in a way he machinated—the Austrian Anschluss. His Luftwaffe had shown itself to be extremely powerful when displayed in the Spanish civil war. He was the public poseur and display agent of the Third Reich. And beneath the purple waistcoats, his heart stirred to contemplate the successes of his economics program. He had a term for it, "rationalization," which meant achieving the greatest output with the least resources. It was a dangerous ploy and in the end it would hurt, because it penalized research for the future, but for the moment it had a shine to it. Even as

Goering, in his capacity as president of the Reichstag, presided over the passage of laws that limited the freedom of Germans generally and destroyed that of the Jews, he was rationalizing everything he did as serving the interests of the German people. Indeed, he was always convinced that, with the possible exception of Hitler, he, Goering, was the true hero of the Nazi movement and that in half a century statues would be erected to him all across Germany for what he had done for the country in the 1930s.

10

BUILDING THE WAR MACHINE

Hermann Goering married for the second time in the spring of 1935. The bride was Emmy Sonnemann, the actress with whom he had been living for the past few months. The wedding was a lavish affair, described bitingly by British Ambassador Sir Eric Phipps as carrying all the trappings of a royal wedding.

As a social commentator the ambassador was on a par with a *Daily Express* gossip columnist. He wrote sarcastically to the Foreign Office: "General Goering would thus seem to have reached the apogee of his vainglorious career. I see for him and his megalomania no higher goal, apart from the throne . . . unless it be the scaffold."

Sir Eric (and most of the rest of the world) missed the real point of what was going on in Germany. A month before the wedding Goering had dropped the mask. His pilots had been training secretly, in the Soviet Union and in Italy, for months. Now they were skilled fighting men, and all they needed was the organization of their air force and the aircraft to fly. Under cover, Goering had both, down to the fine point of the new uniform for the Luftwaffe, which he had designed. And as Goering and his bride honeymooned in Bavaria and

Yugoslavia, the new air force was unveiled to the world. Sir Eric was flabbergasted and again missed the mark wildly; having painted Goering as a buffoon, he now claimed that the German air force had 2,500 first-line aircraft. In fact, there were perhaps 500 military planes.

But Hitler promised Goering that the money and the matériel would be made available and told him that in a year he must have a really strong air force, because the Führer was making ready to reoccupy the Rhineland and he wanted his Luftwaffe to buzz like angry bees and not like a handful of houseflies.

That summer two new aircraft were delivered to Colonel Udet, the director of technical services of the Luftwaffe. They were prototypes of a new weapon. In 1934 Udet had traveled to the United States to participate in a number of air races and had made a careful although unostentatious study of the latest in American aircraft design. He had been particularly impressed by the Curtiss Hawk, which the U.S. Navy had bought in quantity for its aircraft carriers as a dive-bomber and had named the Helldiver. Udet ordered two of them for Germany, and when he returned to Berlin he began experimenting with them and with the design. Secretly, because this was 1934 and the secret was not yet out, he made arrangements with the Junkers company to build a pair of aircraft to his new design, and in the summer of 1935 they were ready to show off. Udet demonstrated them to General Milch and Goering, who was very much impressed with the speed of this bomber, but characteristically demanded a little bit more.

What was the plane called, Goering wanted to know. The Stuka dive-bomber, said Udet.

It was too bad it did not make more noise, said Goering.

The psychological effect of the plane was good, but if it made more noise it could paralyze the enemy.

That was easy enough, said Udet. All they had to do was put a wind whistle on the plane and it would screech like a wildcat as it came thundering down. And that was done. Even Goering was mightily pleased. He told Hitler that he now had one of the most effective weapons in modern air warfare.

In March 1936 the Luftwaffe was ready when Hitler said the great day had come. General Walther Wever, the Luftwaffe chief of staff, was planning to build a force of heavy bombers, but at that time the major effort was on twin-engine medium bombers, the Dornier and the Ju-52. The Horst Wessel fighter squadron had been unveiled to the world in 1935, and soon Germany would boast some 1,800 military aircraft, and Heinkel and Messerschmitt were both working on what came to be the fastest fighter planes in the world.

At the turn of the year Hitler had warned his generals of his intentions. General von Blomberg had predicted gloomily that the action might stir up the British and the French, and that if they mobilized, Germany would have to back down. But Hitler did not believe the British and French were morally and psychologically capable as nations of taking a strong stand, and as it turned out, he was right.

On 7 March 1936 German troops marched into the Rhineland in defiance of the Versailles treaty. Overhead flew the squadrons of fighter planes and bombers, as the trucks and tanks of the mechanized troops rumbled through the villages and towns—and nothing happened.

In July 1935, at the town of Mililla in Spanish Morocco, several generals had rebelled against the Spanish Republican government, which was too far to the left for their liking. Soon General Francisco Franco emerged as generalissimo, and a bloody civil war began. From the outset, Benito Mussolini in Italy supported the Franco rebels with guns, planes and pilots, and by autumn Hitler had jumped onto that bandwagon and recognized the Franco government as the legitimate government of Spain.

The Soviet Union gave assistance to the Spanish Loyalists, and this caused the Italians and the Germans to give even more to the Nationalists. When the Italians sent some seventy-five thousand troops to help Franco, General von Blomberg was not willing to match that sort of help, but Goering was eager to test his new war machine. That was the major reason for German participation in the Spanish civil war: not ideological but practical. Spain was the shooting ground for Luftwaffe target practice. Goering clothed all this in bombastic statements about the "need to prevent the spread of Communism," but he did not really worry about the spread of Communism as Hitler did. (In fact, in the Reichstag days, Goering found it quite compatible to cooperate with the Communists whenever he saw that their interests were the same.)

At a conference between Hitler, von Blomberg and Goering, it was agreed that Germany would send planes and pilots to Spain to fight with Franco. And so in 1936 the Luftwaffe went into military action, German fighter pilots in the air against Russian fighter pilots, while German bombers plastered Madrid and other Loyalist centers with high explosives.

The Germans called themselves the Kondor Legion. The officers and men were "on leave" from the Luftwaffe to volunteer in Spain, but their work was carefully supervised. Goering particularly wanted his ground crews to gain experience, so many more men were sent to service and arm the aircraft than were needed. And back in Germany such factories as the Junkers plant at Dessau were busily turning out Ju-52 bombers and Stukas.

Goering had one setback in the spring of 1936. General Wever died in May, leaving an enormous hole in the Luftwaffe organization. Goering was very busy just then, with the Four-Year Plan for the economy and in the posts he had collected over recent years. General Albert Kesselring was appointed chief of staff, but Kesselring had no talent for this sort of close work, and the Luftwaffe organization suffered accordingly. It was not long before he was transferred to operational duty, for which he was much better suited. Within the year, General Hans-Jürgen Stumpff succeeded Kesselring in the staff post.

In 1938 Hitler began preparing for possible war in Europe. He knew what he wanted, and the first part of it was a combination of two of his aims: to bring all German-speaking peoples under the flag of the Third Reich and to redress the wrongs Germans had suffered at Versailles. That meant bringing Austria into Greater Germany and then getting rid of Czechoslovakia, created out of the Habsburg empire, and unifying the German territory in the north where it had been chopped up for the benefit of Poland.

Preparation for the annexation of Austria and the destruction of Czechoslovakia of course meant that the military forces had to grow very fast. The air force was awarded a third of the military budget these days. Von Blomberg said this was too much, but Hitler disagreed. He demanded that the Luftwaffe be increased fivefold by 1940. The goal was impossible, but Goering and Milch tried to satisfy Hitler by playing the numbers game. They drew plans for the production of six thousand planes and actually produced more than five thousand aircraft, but only thirty-three hundred of them were combat planes, a fact conveniently overlooked by Hitler and the world.

At the same time Goering's control of the German economy was directed toward the nation's imminent move toward war. Having seen the economic recovery of the country, the German people were talking about a better life, but it was not to be. The resources of Germany were to be turned to more armament. Goering's task was to create *Tiefrüstung*—armament in depth—to sustain the Nazi military machine for a long time, and to do so Germany must be made free of dependence on foreign supplies.

Thus, from 1937 government expenditure began to rise sharply. Goering suggested that, if private industry could not manage to produce what he wanted, the government would take over all industry. Already he was taking over the assets and operations of Jewish firms—in order, he said, to keep these companies in the public interest and not allow them to be used by private individuals to satisfy private greed. He proposed the systematic expropriation of Jewish firms under his control in the Four-Year Plan.

HINTS OF THE HOLOCAUST

In Vienna, the streets were daubed with anti-Jewish signs and glass from the smashed windows of Jewish shops piled up in the gutters. It was rumored that 7,000 Jews had committed suicide since the Nazis had arrived, and the Gestapo persecutions had begun.

—Leonard Mosley, *Reich Marshal*

After Austria was annexed, in 1938 Goering supervised the closing down of fourteen thousand Jewish shops and the sale of three thousand more, all in the Nazi interest.

Further, Goering began to put the Ruhr industries under his control and in 1937 created a new superindustry, the Reichswerke Hermann Goering, a state-owned and state-controlled industrial complex. Its capital was at first 5 million marks, but that was soon increased to 400 million marks, and Goering planned that it would become the core of German industry, especially in its output of steel: production must be tripled, even quadrupled. By 1939 he had accomplished that aim, mainly by exploitation of the large supply of low-grade iron ores in southern and central Germany.

One of the opponents of Goering's scheme was General von Blomberg, the war minister. When Goering found himself unable to persuade von Blomberg, he decided to get rid of him. And he did so very shrewdly. Von Blomberg sought Goering's assistance in a matter of the heart. His wife had died and he had fallen in love with a much younger woman. But this young woman had several lovers, who were most inconvenient. Goering helped by sending one of them off to a job in Argentina, then he indicated that he would assist von Blomberg in covering up the shady past of his inamorata. Meanwhile he was using his broad espionage system, developed as head of the Prussian police, to gather a complete dossier on von Blomberg and the woman. When it was finished, he informed Hitler of the facts, and Hitler erupted, as Goering knew he would, in righteous indignation against von Blomberg's "immorality." Von Blomberg was forced to resign his commission and thus was effectively removed as war minister and as an opponent of Hermann Goering.

Although by the end of 1937 Goering was hoping to be made minister of war, and thus to have the responsibility for all Germany's armed forces, the Führer took over the war ministry for himself. Goering was created field marshal, but it was still hard to swallow the defeat. Still, he was now the highest-ranking officer in all the armed forces, and that counted for something.

Success went to his head, but not as badly as some believed. The other climbers on the ladder were only too eager to believe the worst of Goering, and to arrange his downfall if they could. He was universally envied, Alfred Rosenberg hated him and Rudolf Hess was enormously jealous, so much so that he tried to suppress all publicity about Goering—which was impossible, of course. Himmler and his friends bided their time, but they, too, hated Goering.

So the years of war approached, and Hitler knew that his deputy had done a good job of preparing Germany for conflict. Germany, said the leadership, was now ready for war. The economy had been tamed and turned to Nazi purposes. The German people had been made ready for war and were welcoming it.

Goering was not only the most powerful man in the Third Reich except for Hitler, he was without doubt the most popular. He had tamed the army and the industrialists, and he had even made friends for himself and for Germany in faraway places. Even among the British there were a certain number of political leaders who believed that Goering, unlike Hitler, was a man they could trust. It just shows how little they really knew, for Goering was not only the No. 2 Nazi, courtesy of Hitler's dictum, but also No. 2 in adherence to the Nazi theories. He went with the Führer every step of the way.

In 1937 Goering's concept of a new Germany was complete. He and Hitler had discussed this matter a number of times; who influenced whom is not really known, but by this year their views were remarkably similar.

Goering first wanted to achieve a superstate of "Mitteleuropa"—Central Europe. Austria would be the first part of it, and then the German-speaking areas of Czechoslovakia—its Slav areas, which Goering found inimical to German interests, would be colonies, not part of the Greater Reich. Poland, too, would be dismembered, with the Germanic elements becoming part of Germany and the non-Germanic Poles colonized. Russia was to be de-Sovietized and made a dependency.

In the west, Britain was to be isolated and kept out of European affairs, and France was to be reduced to dependency on Germany and Italy, her ally.

The racial aspect of all this change was not very important in Goering's thinking, but it was the cornerpost of Hitler's. Thus, as was shown time and again by Goering in his personal life, although he had no antipathy to Jews, he would never controvert Hitler in this matter.

Privately he agreed with Emmy Sonnemann that Jews were just like all other people (but a little smarter, Goering said). In his personal relations he had long ago decided to ignore the question of race. He certainly preferred the company of many Jews to that of the race-baiting Nazis. When Hitler and Goebbels got onto the subject of Jews, it made Goering nervous, and he usually escaped the conversation by going somewhere else on urgent business. So we see a Goering who has sacrificed morality from the beginning. His godfather, his childhood hero, was a Jew.

From as early as 1935, Goering could not blind himself to

the anti-Semitism of the Nazi government. No matter his private views and despite the economic motives of his own actions against Jewish property, his acceptance of the racial policy made his guilt as great as anyone's.

His wife, Emmy Sonnemann, had many Jewish friends who were getting into trouble. He bailed a number of them out of trouble with the Gestapo and SS (though he complained to Emmy that she made life difficult for him) and gained a reputation in liberal circles as being secretly a friend to the Jews. But there was no real truth in it. He accepted the letter and the spirit of the Nuremberg laws restricting the rights of Jews, and there is no indication that even once did he question the Führer's actions or words regarding Jews. Goering's main concern regarding the Jews was that their expropriated holdings be used in the service of the Third Reich and not dribble into the pockets of Nazi officials; it was certainly not a concern for the Jews or their well-being.

For example, when Goebbels roused the rabble of the SA and SS on that terrible evening in November 1938 known as *Kristallnacht,* Goering was furious, not because the Jews were being mistreated but because the burning out of the Jews would mean big payments to be made by German insurance companies (under Goering's command) and that their own property could not be used to further the ends of the Four-Year Plan. Goering complained to Hitler, who put him in charge of the problem of dealing with the Jews, and systematically Goering began stripping them of their property. He promised to solve the problem by the end of 1938 by removing the Jews completely as factors in the German economy. He very nearly managed to reach that goal.

LEGALIZED PERSECUTION

Effective January 1, 1939, Jews shall be prohibited from operating retail stores and wholesale establishments, as well as independent workshops. They shall be further prohibited from keeping employees or offering any ready-made products on the market; from advertising or receiving orders. Whenever a Jewish shop is operated the police shall shut it down. . . .

—Funk at Kristallnacht

In Vienna, too, when the Austrian Nazis were about to take over some seventeen thousand Jewish shops, and he learned that they were waiting for his decree to do so, he rushed in to give it to them. Later, when much of Europe was occupied, Goering worked closely with the SS and the Gestapo to expropriate Jewish property for his Four-Year Plan.

When Hitler began moving against Austria in 1938, Goering played an important role, but when Hitler moved against Czechoslovakia, Goering was in the wings. What he did do during this period was continue to build the Luftwaffe and to make excellent propaganda for Germany about her invincible military strength, at a time when Germany was really *not* invincible. This was concealed from the British and the French by much bombast and many show trips for officers to see what Goering wanted them to see, which did not include the holes in the Siegfried Line or the shortages of various types of military aircraft in the Luftwaffe.

"Come out and see our exercises and visit our factories," he invited the visiting generals. "We have nothing to hide."

What they saw, of course, was a handful of the most modern aircraft and the most skillful pilots, with an indication that behind this spearhead was unlimited power, when actually it was largely a cardboard façade. And the foreigners were almost always impressed by Goering's geniality and the indication of great strength. America's Charles A. Lindbergh went away awed with German air power and visibly impressed by Goering. Thereafter Lindbergh became a prime mover in the "America First" campaign, which was dedicated to keeping the United States out of war with Germany.

At this point, Goering kept betting his friends that there would not be a war. There was no need for war, he said. If Hitler would leave matters to him, he could guarantee that there would be no war, and still Germany would have what she needed for protection and expansion.

But Goering's task in 1938 was to prepare Germany economically and the Luftwaffe physically for war. There was much to be done. By August 1938 the German air force possessed only two-thirds of the authorized air-crew strength. For example, 1,400 bomber crews were authorized, but only 378 were fully operational. Such shortages existed in every aspect of the Luftwaffe. The fact was that, had the Western powers risen up in the matter of Czechoslovakia, neither the army nor the air force was ready to fight. But so deft had been Goering's propaganda, particularly with the French, who spread it to the British, that the Western powers believed the German air force to be well-nigh invincible.

However, as the operating generals knew, Germany's ability to attack Britain was "no more than to deliver a series of pinpricks." One general suggested that even by 1940 the Luftwaffe would not have a single air division capable of sustaining attack.

So Goering and his generals devised a new strategy to

ABANDONED

Actually the whole thing was a cut-and-dried affair. Neither Chamberlain nor Daladier were in the least bit interested in sacrificing or risking anything to save Czechoslovakia.

—Goering

---

make best use of their limited resources: the air force would depend upon the army. The Luftwaffe would destroy the enemy air force and would support army ground operations. No longer was there talk that the Luftwaffe could win the war single-handedly, as Goering had once boasted to Hitler. But many people in high places in the West still believed it.

By 1938 Goering had consolidated his political power in Germany, but his economic power was not undisputed: the army kept trying to break into the cordon; Wilhelm Keppler, Hitler's economist, tried to break through; so did Robert Ley, the man in charge of the Reich's labor force; but none of them succeeded. Biographer R. J. Overy has suggested that Goering "had a shrewd sense of how to exploit the gap between Hitler's fantasy and German reality." In other words, Hitler was the dreamer, and Goering was the pragmatist who made the Third Reich work as a viable government.

Goering had several advantages. During 1936 and 1937 he had come out against the corruption of the cartels and big business, which appealed to the German masses. The press was mostly on his side, and Goebbels was so successful in trumpeting the changes of the new economy that foreign economists began to believe that the Third Reich's prosperity was real, that somehow the Germans were becoming victorious over the laws of supply and demand. To all, the Four-Year economic plan seemed successful, so much so that Adolf Hitler had no qualms about preparing for the war through which he hoped to conquer Europe and destroy the Soviet Union.

"The Four-Year Plan has the task of preparing the German economy for total war," said Goering. This meant the integration of the economies of the captive territories into the Reich economy, for the best interests of Germany. But the problem for Goering in 1939 was that the planning envisaged that total war to come in 1946, not in 1939, and Hitler was rushing matters. Even to be ready by 1946 meant a constant lowering of the living standards of the German people, which Goering recognized would happen even in 1938.

In 1939 Hitler—not Goering—decided that the air force must be expanded to include heavy bombers, to bring enemies to their knees through strategic bombing. Goering was responsible for this decision in a way, for he had always told Hitler that air power could win a war for them, but it was Hitler who became the enthusiast now, operating on his usual "hunches." Development of the He-177 heavy bomber was pressed that year, with a force of more than two thousand bombers to be ready in the middle 1940s, capable of carrying the war even to America. In the interim the Germans would have to rely on the Ju-88 medium bomber, which was in production. By 1945 Germany expected to have five thousand medium bombers as well as the heavy bombers.

In order to carry out the Four-Year Plan, Hitler decided that he would have to speed up the acquisition of territories needed to supplement the Third Reich's assets. He must solve the Polish problem and secure the return of Danzig and Prussian Poland to Germany. Then Germany could arm to face the west and the east. Hitler was supremely confident after Munich that the British and the French would not fight for Poland or any other territory except their own, and he was willing to wait three or four years before attacking them.

One day in the spring of 1939, while taking a walk with Goering, Hitler suddenly announced that he intended to solve the Polish problem within the next few months. He would make a threat of force, but he was sure the Poles would capitulate, as had the Czechs and Slovaks, and that once more he would have his way. The important matter, he told Goering, was to eliminate the Polish problem without the threat of a general European war.

NO TURNING BACK

The die was now fully and truly cast. Goering knew that his Fuehrer was determined to execute Operation White, the attack on Poland.

—Asher Lee, *Goering: Air Leader*

11

THE COURSE OF EMPIRE

If the Germans had won World War II, what sort of world would have emerged? One thing is certain: the Soviet Union would have been one great German colony, supplying slave labor. Another surmise that is not so well known is that Germany would have taken over large sectors of the British Empire.

The father of that idea was Hermann Goering. It was quite natural for him to think thus, for his father had been a colonial official in the old German Empire, governor of the Cameroons for a time, and had held high posts in other colonies in Africa.

"Wir wollen ein Reich," he used to say. "We want an Empire." How would it be created?

By 1939, without war, the Germans had made a good beginning. Austria had acquiesced quietly, and so had Bohemia and Moravia; Slovakia was a different matter—Hitler distrusted all Slavs—and it would remain independent as long as the Slovaks did Hitler's bidding. If they ever stopped, they would be made into slaves.

Goering had a great deal to do with these changes, although his part in the Czechoslovak matter is obscured by his quarreling with von Ribbentrop, who liked to take personal credit for everything.

As early as 1935 Hitler had given Goering special responsibilities in the field of foreign relations.

Foreign policy to the Third Reich was not just a ministry managed by an official; it was inherent in all the Nazis did, and the chief agents of the foreign policy were Hitler, the theoretician, and Goering, the practical politician. (Through his own intelligence agencies, he knew what was happening in the world far more clearly than did Hitler.) The mechanics were left to the specialists, Freiherr Konstantin von Neurath in the beginning, and then Joachim von Ribbentrop and Franz von Papen, but the control was largely in Goering's hands, particularly in the cases of Austria and Italy. (Italy became one of Goering's responsibilities because of Hitler's mistaken notion that Goering had a special relationship with Mussolini dating from the days when Goering had been a fugitive from Germany.)

When Goering traveled to Italy to confer with Mussolini, he assured the Italians that Germany would not move single-handedly in Austria, though all the while he was planning to just that end. However, Goering was already setting up the conditions favorable to the Austrian Anschluss. As head of the Four-Year Plan, he was able to make special tariff and trade agreements with the Austrians and to award the contracts to firms that showed themselves friendly to the Nazis. This was the sort of work at which he excelled.

It was Goering, not Hitler, who took charge of the negotiations with Austria early in March 1938, and these negotiations led to the resignation of Chancellor Schuschnigg and his cabinet. During the Austrian cabinet crisis, Goering spent most of two days in a telephone booth talking to the Austrian Nazi leaders whom he had personally egged on during the previous few weeks. He managed the resignation of Schuschnigg, and that of the Austrian president, and the invitation to Germany to send troops across the border. To be sure, Hitler played the grand master at Berchtesgaden, but the engineering was done by Goering. For example, by 1937 he had the Austrian foreign minister, Guido Schmitt, safely in his pocket, and after the Anschluss Schmitt was employed as supervisor of Austria's Four-Year Plan. Once the Austrian state was integrated into the Third Reich, Goering lost no time in also integrating every element of the economy. Vienna was reduced in political status to a provincial capital, and the Austrian economy was so carefully integrated into the German that it was hard to believe they had ever been separate countries.

In the breakup of Czechoslovakia, it was Goering's aim to separate out all the Germanic elements, which he found compatible with the economic aims of the Third Reich. He favored Slovakian "independence" because it would put the Czechs at the Germans' mercy. In 1938 he made several trips to Budapest and Warsaw, in order to secure Hungarian and Polish support for the dissection of Czechoslovakia. Both countries were frightened, because both contained German-speaking minorities, and they did not know when Hitler might move against them. Had he not written in *Mein Kampf* that he intended to bring all German-speaking peoples under the roof of the Third Reich? Indeed he had, but Goering blandly promised the Hungarians and the Poles that, if they would support the dismemberment of that "inconceivable monstrosity, Czechoslovakia, even its name comes apart," this would be the Germans' last territorial demand. (As Goering said these words with broad smiles, he already knew Hitler's plans for Poland, and he was very much a part of the preparations.) So Hungary and Poland went along in support of Germany on the Czechoslovak question.

The only difference between Goering and von Ribbentrop on the Czechoslovak problem was method. Von Ribbentrop believed in threatening with the sword and being prepared for general war. Goering, who knew much more about war than von Ribbentrop, favored the easier method of economic destruction. He had the power and the will to use it to get what Hitler wanted. Hitler, who was inclined to go along with von Ribbentrop, was convinced by Goering to try the peaceful route, and saw how well it worked. First the Sudeten Germans were brought into camp, and then Goering began the economic strangulation of what was left of Czechoslovakia, weakening it to the point at which the Germans had their way about war. His method was to force a customs and currency union on the Czechs. Skoda and other companies were flooded with orders for arms from the Germans, and by the spring of 1939 the formal dismemberment of Czechoslovakia did not make a stir in the economic situation.

In the late 1930s many people of goodwill in Europe believed that somehow war could be prevented, but the fact was that only if Europe was willing to submit to enslavement without war could it have been prevented. Everything Hermann Goering did, from brandishing the Luftwaffe under the noses of Europe and sharpening that weapon in the Spanish civil war, to forcible integration of the economies of all the "new" German areas, was an integral part of the German drive for empire. At the Nuremberg war-crimes trials, he made a good case for himself and half-convinced some of those in attendance that he had not been a moving factor, but the fact was that he was responsible for many of Hitler's ideas about dealing with people outside the Nazi structure. Hitler, after all, never traveled abroad. His only knowledge was of Germany and Austria. Goering was a man of the world.

Goering had planned from the beginning to put the Germans on short rations and demand more work from them as the price they must pay to achieve the great new German empire. In the ten years ending in 1938, wages dropped, national consumption of goods dropped and standards of living went down.

PRIORITIES

What does your production for the home market mean in comparison with the interests of the nation?

—Goering

Goering's standard of living did not, of course. He still feasted on pheasant, and pâté de foie gras and caviar, and if rebuked about it (which virtually no one had the courage to do) he would say that rank has its privileges.

In 1938, the Four-Year Plan was changed to prepare Germany for a long "total war" with the West. This meant that Goering had to arrange not only the integration of the economies of captive territories into that of the Reich but for supplies of raw materials from the Balkan states and Scandinavia. As noted elsewhere, his personal influence with the Swedes persuaded them to go along with Germany and thus save themselves from the sort of occupation suffered by the Norwegians and the Danes.

One does not usually associate Hermann Goering with

railroads, but he was the man responsible for the complete reorganization of the German rail system in the 1930s to meet the needs of the military, so great was his power in the Third Reich, so all-pervasive the Four-Year Plan.

Germany was preparing for war, that was certain, but the fact was that she did not want war until 1944 or later—that was Goering's timetable, for the railroads, for the mechanization of the army, for the completion of a strategic bombing force of two thousand heavy bombers. All this was knocked aside because of Hitler's whimsicality. He had been prepared for war with Czechoslovakia. He had learned, to his surprise at first, that Britain and France would not fight, and then he had become contemptuous of them and certain that they would never fight. That is why the war came in Poland in 1939. Hitler thought the Allies were bluffing, when they were not at all, and he started a war five years before anyone else in Germany wanted it. Even von Ribbentrop, one of the most radical of the Nazis, wanted to wait three or four more years before embarking on a general European war.

In that summer of 1939 the idea was to isolate Poland, be sure that the Soviets and the British did not get involved, and then take over the Poles. Their industrial and labor capacities would be extremely helpful in speeding up the Third Reich's armament program.

Von Ribbentrop was given the task of taking out the Soviets, and Goering that of persuading the British not to intervene. Goering was always a favorite with visiting British delegations, and Hitler had the idea that Goering had more influence with the British than any other man in the Third Reich, especially himself, for after Munich the diplomats had begun to distrust Hitler, and he knew it.

At the last, when all Goering's efforts to placate the British had failed, he was truly shocked. When he learned that the

British had declared war, he picked up the telephone in his Berlin office and called von Ribbentrop.

"Well," he said, "I hope you're satisfied. Now you've got your damned war."

12

BLITZKRIEG!

The reason for Goering's shock when he heard the news that Britain and Germany were at war was that he had thought he could manage the British, that he had some special relationship with them that in the end would save the day.

In order to localize the coming conflict with Poland, in the spring of 1939 Hitler had sought nonaggression treaties with Britain and the Soviet Union. Goering, who had great respect for the British, was very pleased when he was asked to take over negotiations, replacing the ministrations of Foreign Minister von Ribbentrop's Foreign Office. But the matter was complicated by von Ribbentrop's dislike for Goering and by the foreign minister's attempts to increase his own stature in the government.

When it became apparent that the normal diplomatic channels were producing no accord with Britain, Hitler asked Goering informally to assure Britain that the Germans had no designs on her empire. The idea was to detach Britain from France.

Goering then began buttering up the British.

"At this time," he claimed later, at the Nuremberg trials, "I was in touch with Lord Halifax by special courier outside the regular diplomatic channels." He invited the British ambassador to go stag hunting. He spoke of economic concessions the Third Reich would make to the British in matters of trade. British representatives came to Berlin in August, and Goering impressed them as being a man of business and "goodwill." This was precisely the impression he wished to leave, in order to persuade the British to make the same sort of concessions while Germany swallowed Poland as they had when Germany swallowed Czechoslovakia.

Goering was meticulous in his work here, because he wanted to make sure that he gained the credit with Hitler. He was still smarting from von Ribbentrop's claim of credit for the German-Italian alliance, which, in fact, Goering had suggested and promoted before von Ribbentrop came onto the scene.

But despite Goering's best efforts, he learned from his intelligence sources that they were not going to do any good in this case. The British were determined to live up to their alliance with Poland. This became apparent in August, and when it did, Goering consulted Hitler, and Hitler delayed the invasion of Poland.

That happened on August 25. That was the day on which Ambassador Henderson told Hitler that the British would most certainly live up to their commitment to Poland. Hitler did not believe it even yet—he was so used to having his own way, with the Western leaders backing down. So he sent new messages to London and hoped for the best.

But that afternoon a new Anglo-Polish alliance was signed in London that gave absolute proof to the British contention that it would support Warsaw's independence, and Hitler suddenly got cold feet. He called General Keitel to the Chancellery and told the chief of staff to stop the movements of troops toward Poland. He told Keitel to get von Brauchitsch, the commander of the Wehrmacht, because he had to buy some time for negotiation.

Hitler called Goering on the telephone and told him he had stopped the invasion. Goering asked if that was permanent. No, said Hitler, it was just a pause to see if somehow he could not persuade the British to forgo war.

Goering then began some last-minute negotiations with the British.

There was a considerable background to this decision, and to the events that followed. It all stemmed from Hitler's belief that the British would not fight. He talked about settling for the return of Danzig and the Polish Corridor, for good arguments could be advanced here. Birger Dahlerus, a Swedish businessman who was a friend of Goering's of long standing, entered the negotiations to try to stop war. After a series of messages, Dahlerus came to Berlin, carrying a letter from Lord Halifax to Goering, because Halifax said he believed Goering was the one German who might be able to stop a war.

So Goering received the letter from Dahlerus, while the field marshal was on a train to his Luftwaffe headquarters at Oranienburg, outside Berlin. He stopped the train and commandeered a car in which he took Dahlerus to Berlin. They went to the Chancellery. It was dark. Hitler had gone to bed. Goering insisted on waking him up and introduced the Swede.

Hitler was in a foul mood, as Dahlerus later recalled:

> *Hitler listened without interrupting, but then suddenly got up and, becoming very excited and nervous, walked up and down saying as though to himself that Germany was irresistible. Suddenly*

he stopped in the middle of the room and stood there staring.

His voice was blurred and his behavior was that of a completely abnormal person. He spoke in staccato phrases:

"If there should be war, then I shall build U-boats, build U-boats, U-boats." His voice became more indistinct and finally one could not follow him at all. Then he pulled himself together, raised his voice as though addressing a large audience and shrieked: "I shall build airplanes, build airplanes, airplanes, airplanes, and I shall annihilate my enemies." He seemed more like a phantom from a storybook than a real person. I stared at him in amazement and turned to see how Goering was reacting. . . . [William L. Shirer, *The Rise and Fall of the Third Reich*]

Goering was not reacting at all. He was quite used to Hitler's flights into the world of fantasy and fury. He had been seeing them for fifteen years.

As for the letter from Lord Halifax, it was a long while before it was remembered. Then Hitler calmed down and dealt with the matter. Dahlerus was sent back to London with a six-point plan for peace: Germany wanted an alliance with Britain. She wanted help to regain Danzig and the Polish Corridor, she was to have her pre–World War I colonies back, and she would in turn pledge herself to defend the British Empire.

For some reason, Hitler thought he had so frightened the British in the past that a pledge to defend the British Empire would be welcomed. Instead, it was seen in London as the arrogant ploy it really was.

Aside from the pledge, Goering had initiated most of the items in the offer, and he thought it would work. He made Dahlerus commit the terms to memory, for it was too delicate a matter to put on paper.

For a week Goering and Dahlerus negotiated, in meetings and by telephone.

Nevile Henderson, the British Ambassador, was convinced that Goering was a man of peace who was really trying to settle affairs. But von Ribbentrop and the other radicals argued that, with the Nazi-Soviet pact, the Germans need have no fear of the British and that Hitler ought to march into war with Poland to achieve his ends.

Goering's argument very nearly won Poland without a fight. The British government was doing just what he wanted that August, pressing the Poles to accept the return of Danzig and the Corridor, and concessions to the German minority in Poland. Goering had earlier arranged several meetings with British businessmen, and on August 19 he and Hitler agreed that it was worthwhile for Goering to make a special secret mission to Britain, to persuade the British to help Germany as Neville Chamberlain had in the Czechoslovak crisis. It was all settled. Goering was to fly to Britain on August 23. He would land at a small airfield near Bovingdon in Hertfordshire and would be driven directly to meet Prime Minister Chamberlain at Chequers, his country house. The Secret Service was making all the arrangements. But the trip did not come off, because on August 21 von Ribbentrop announced that he had made a treaty with the Soviet Union. He had convinced Hitler that, because of that treaty, Germany had nothing to fear from Britain. When von Ribbentrop heard of the Goering trip, he scoffed and told Hitler that there was no sense in it. So Hitler killed the mission. He then made the decision to march, for he was convinced that Britain would not, in the end, go to war over Poland.

Hitler met his senior military officers to announce the plans for Poland. Four days later he wrote to Mussolini to tell him that he was moving. He recorded his decision in the *Hitler Papers.*

"As neither France nor Britain can achieve any decisive successes in the west, and as Germany, as result of the agreement with Russia, will have all her forces free in the east after the defeat of Poland, and as air superiority is undoubtedly on our side, I do not shrink from solving the eastern question even at the risk of complications with the west."

So in the early hours of 1 September 1939, German bombers and fighters began to deliver attacks on targets in Poland. Goering had hoped to give a quick knockout blow to Polish military installations and armament factories, but bad weather prevented such an attack that first day. So the Luftwaffe for the most part planned to confine its efforts to close support of the army.

For a week the German war machine was in position, waiting nervously along the Polish border. Army Group North consisted of the Third and Fourth Armies. Army Group South consisted of the Eighth, Tenth and Fourteenth Armies. In East Prussia the Third Army was also ready to march. The spearhead of General Fedor von Bock's Army Group North was General Heinz Guderian's XIX Panzer Corps.

The Third Army would march on Warsaw. Then the southern force would march on Cracow, and the northern force would move to crush the Poles between the nutcracker jaws.

One new element: the army expected and would get close air support from the Luftwaffe in the initial operations. General Albert Kesselring was in charge of the 1st and 4th Air Fleets. He was assisted by General Alexander Löhr and General Wolfram von Richthofen, a veteran of the Spanish campaigns.

The actuality on September 1 was almost an anticlimax, because for six days the Luftwaffe had been waiting. On the night of August 25 the Luftwaffe was ready. The bombers were loaded and the fighters were prepared to take off. But that night came word from Berlin: "Hold up." And so, for the next six days the armies waited on the Polish border, and the pilots fretted, waiting for orders. When the word came, early on September 1, the bombers were off and heading for their targets. The Dornier 17s carried clusters of hundred-pound antipersonnel bombs. The Stukas carried five-hundred-pound bombs. They made their attacks on Polish planes lined up neatly on the runways of the airfields, on infantry, artillery and cavalry marching in neat columns down the roads. The effect was terrible. In minutes the roads were scenes of devastation and carnage. It was a case of a modern war machine fighting a nineteenth-century army.

At 4:45 that morning, the Luftwaffe sent out 1,929 aircraft. The attacks were aimed mainly against the Polish airfields. They demolished Cracow Airport and much of the Polish air force stationed there. The Stukas were particularly effective against the Polish army, which, in its columns on the roads, was easy prey for the screaming bombers. One whole brigade was knocked out in an hour. In forty-eight hours the Polish air force had ceased to exist. The five hundred first-line planes had mostly been destroyed on the ground by German bombers.

On the land, the Poles had organized their defenses along the Polish Corridor and in Silesia. They were easy prey for the German armies, and the air force.

At 10 A.M. on September 5 General von Brauchitsch and General von Bock conferred and agreed that the attack had virtually defeated the Poles already. Von Kluge's Fourth Army from Pomerania and von Kühler's Third Army from East Prussia had met. General Guderian's panzers had met the Polish Pomorska Cavalry Brigade in the Corridor and had massacred them. It was cavalryman against tank, with the Stukas roaring overhead. Within the first ten days, General Walther von Reichenau's Tenth Army had broken out into the plains.

Cracow fell on September 6. That night the Polish government abandoned threatened Warsaw and moved to Lublin. The next day the fate of Poland was so certain that the high command in Berlin decided to transfer excess troops to the western front just in case the British and French might be up to something.

Tanks were halfway to Warsaw on the sixth day of the campaign, and everywhere that Polish forces moved they were harried by the Stukas and the German fighters. General Guderian's tanks, supported by Goering's planes, cut through the Polish army like a knife through cheese. The 4th Panzer Division moved into the outskirts of Warsaw on September 8. In a week the Polish army was decimated. Most of the thirty-five divisions were gone. The Germans were moving to surround the Polish units west of Brest-Litovsk and the River Bug. A major Polish force was isolated on the Bzura River, surrounded and then bombed repeatedly by the Luftwaffe. The Stuka, indeed, proved to be the fearsome weapon that Goering had said. The screaming dive paralyzed many troops, and they threw away their weapons and ran.

General von Richthofen, given the responsibility for attacking Warsaw, said he proposed to destroy the city so completely that it would thereafter be useful only "as a customs station." He proceeded to try to do just this.

By the end of September the Polish army was gone, and so was the air force. The Poles had lost 70,000 men dead, 133,000 wounded and 700,000 prisoners of war. Total German casualties were fewer than 50,000.

But three weeks after the attack on Poland, Britain and France responded with declarations of war on Germany, and the Luftwaffe had a new responsibility to carry out.

The air war in the west began as a war of reconnaissance. The Germans did not bomb land targets, but they did begin looking for British convoys and ships and attacking them.

By September 17 almost all Polish troops were surrounded. The Polish government reached the Romanian border. In Berlin, the Nazis were making plans to partition Poland and share it with the Russians. But the war in the west was very quiet, and soon the guns stopped popping along the Polish front.

At this point the Luftwaffe had more than four thousand aircraft. So pleased was Hitler with the performance of Goering's men in the Polish campaign that he predicted a great future: the Luftwaffe might win the war single-handedly for him, he joked. And he set his plans for the attack on the west; the first step would be an offensive to harm the Allied armies as much as possible, but basically to set the stage for air and sea attacks on Britain. The idea was to strike into the heart of British power and at the same time to protect the Ruhr basin from similar attacks by the enemy.

But on the ground nothing was happening, and in the air it seemed very lazy and lonely. The Germans invented the name for the situation: *Sitzkrieg*—the sit-down war.

That was the war that existed on the western front in the last months of 1939 and the early months of 1940. Everyone seemed to be moving in slow motion. Hitler was moving troops around his chessboard. The Luftwaffe was trying to build strength, and so were France and Britain.

The great difference among them was in their views toward warfare. The Germans, forced to a policy of close ground support of the troops by bad weather in Poland, had made capital of the move, and the Luftwaffe was celebrated through the world as the strongest air force in Europe. The blitzkrieg, forced upon the Germans by the weather and made successful by luck, was seen as the wave of the future in the European war. Altogether, Hermann Goering's rebaptism of fire in 1939 had proved extremely successful.

The Luftwaffe was Germany's most feared weapon, courtesy of Goebbels' propaganda; it was also Germany's most frightening weapon. Soon enough would come the chance for Goering to test his weapon against the major Western powers and to plan the Nazi conquest of Europe and the east.

13

THE PHONEY WAR

No one was more surprised than Hermann Goering at the outcome of the Polish campaign. It created an illusion that no one had expected: the vision of an unbeatable German war machine. The reason was simple enough if anyone thought about it: it was not hard for a modern military machine with armor and air force to defeat an old-fashioned army, but the speed and ease with which the Luftwaffe and the panzers destroyed the Polish army and air force was so phenomenal that the world believed the Germans were much stronger than they were.

The German people were euphoric. Everything Hitler had promised them was coming to pass. As one ardent Nazi youth, Heinz Knöke, wrote in *I Flew for the Führer,* "Want, poverty, unemployment? They have ceased to exist in the Third Reich. Is it so strange, therefore, for Austria to have sought union with a strong and prosperous Reich? It seems only common sense for the people of the Sudeten territory to do the same, and for Memel to seek freedom from Lithuanian rule."

As for Poland, the Nazi propaganda machine said that until August 31 "the Polish atrocities against the German minority make horrible reading. . . . Thousands of Germans are being massacred daily in territory which had once been part of Germany. Thousands more arrive every hour in the Reich, each refugee with another tale of horror."

So, of course, the youth of Germany had been eager to punish Poland, eager to fight. The blitzkrieg was wonderful. The war would be over by Christmas, they were saying in Hamelin and Berlin and Munich. But later—and not so very much later—this easy victory would have its complications. Hitler, having seen success, would not understand the major weaknesses of the Luftwaffe.

The most salient weakness was right at the top. Field Marshal Goering, the chief of the Luftwaffe, was by 1939 much more politician than soldier. His chief function was actually the management of the Reich economy, so that Hitler could have his way. He was extremely busy with his obligations in that area, and consequently the Luftwaffe suffered from inattention.

Hitler publicly proclaimed that Goering was the heir to the Third Reich. Goering made a triumphal train journey into the Polish Corridor and was lionized by the German population—"liberated citizens," they were called in Germany. He went to Warsaw to see the wreckage caused by his Luftwaffe pilots and was himself amazed. The real reason for his trip was to assess the resources newly available to Germany and to waste no time in making use of them. He issued his first directives concerning the diversion of raw materials, the turn of manufacturing companies to make products needed in Germany and the conscription of forced labor to work in German factories.

At the time, Goering justified the speed with which he moved as necessary only for the moment. He really believed that he was going to be able to persuade Britain to stop fighting Germany, and he hoped to accomplish this task in the next few weeks.

When Goering began once more trying to negotiate with the British, he had an excellent weapon in his Swedish connections. Carin's son by her previous marriage, Thomas von Kantzow, had remained loyal and close to Goering since his mother's death. He was now employed by the field marshal as a messenger. He took two letters from British prisoners of war, airmen who had been shot down over Germany, plus a letter from Goering to the RAF assuring them that the men would be looked after, pledging his word as head of the Luftwaffe. These letters were taken to Birger Dahlerus in Stockholm, and he took them on to the British minister. Dahlerus also assured the minister that Goering was the most popular man in Germany (which was true) and that Hitler's popularity was declining (which was probably true but did not make any difference as long as Hitler controlled the Nazi machinery).

The British minister was also told that his country could believe in Goering and that Goering was tired of the war, as were the German people. These statements were quite true, but again, in the face of Hitler, they really did not make a lot of difference. Nor was Goering willing to join in the generals' plot against Hitler; he remained loyal to his chief. He did, however, put more hope in the idea of negotiation with the British than Hitler was now prepared to do, and Goering was willing to achieve a real peace, while all Hitler wanted was respite before continuing his drive to world conquest.

At the end of September, Birger Dahlerus appeared once more in Berlin. He went to Goering's office, and the excited Goering took him to see Hitler. Their mission was to hear Hitler's latest plan for peace—if he had any.

Hitler was not thinking much about peace just then. He

was full of himself and full of plans for further conquest. The glory of Germany was reviving. No longer could he consider the old ideas: the withdrawal from Poland except for Danzig and the Polish Corridor. Now he had all Poland, and he was about to split it up in a deal with the Soviet Union that would give him the Baltic provinces.

So now all the British could salvage, said Hitler, was the security of their own empire and the neutrality of the Netherlands and Belgium. In that case, "the Siegfried Line will be the unalterable west wall of Germany," said the Führer. He assured the Swedish unofficial envoy that the Germans did not want conquests in the west or in the Balkans. His plan for Poland, he said, was to incorporate the Germanic areas into greater Germany and use the rest as an asylum for European Jews.

After one day in Berlin, Birger Dahlerus went to the Netherlands and thence swiftly to Britain with a priority airflight sponsored by the British Embassy. He was greeted warmly at the British Foreign Office, where he discussed Hitler's stance and Goering's hopes. Goering had said he was willing to fly to any neutral capital and meet a British representative there.

But the British government was suspicious of the German government, Dahlerus was finally told at the Foreign Office. The problem was Hitler. After 1 September 1939 no one in Europe believed in Hitler's proclamations of peaceful intentions. One part of the British cabinet hoped that Goering (in whom they did believe) would join the generals (whom the British would not help) and overthrow Hitler.

Another element, more belligerent, properly refused to assume that Goering was disloyal to Hitler. This was the Churchillian element, and the position was simple: Poland must be restored to the Polish government before there could be any discussions of peace.

Dahlerus returned to Germany with the bad news. His best efforts had been rebuffed by the British. Goering was annoyed. He had always known that the British could be stubborn, but now he saw that there was no talking to them at all. In his annoyance he decided that the British must be taught that they were not all-powerful. And in the Luftwaffe, Goering held, he had the instrument to teach them.

The Luftwaffe was expanding, to meet the demands Goering would place upon it. On an autumn day in 1939, a young man named Heinz Knöke left his home in Hamelin to go to Schönewalde Airfield, to join No. 11 Flying Training Regiment. By January 1940 he was in the military academy, and on February 17 he made his first official flight. By April he had completed eighty-three training flights and was soloing.

Goering said his Luftwaffe was now ready to take on all comers. He was eager to send the aircraft west against Britain. He did not seem to know much about the concerns of General Milch: the fighter commanders claimed that the Me-109 was inferior to the British Spitfire, but Goering did not hear. General Milch kept bringing up the subject of heavy bombers to carry out strategic bombing campaigns against distant targets, but Goering's answer was that the Reich did not have the raw materials to build the aircraft just then.

Goering did want to conduct a bombing campaign against Britain which was, in effect, strategic bombing. He told Hitler that he could force the British to reconsider their high-handed approach to peace. He would bomb their airfields and factories. He would paralyze British industry.

British sources later indicated that, if Hitler had agreed, Britain would indeed have faced greater difficulty even than she did, for in the last months of 1939 and the first months of 1940 she was not in a good position to defend herself. The government had responded very slowly to the threat of war in the middle 1930s, and the defense effort was just now getting under way.

But, fortunately for Britain, Hitler did not appreciate strategic bombing. His was the psychology of the immediate. He had a fearsome weapon in the blitzkrieg. He wanted the Luftwaffe's striking power and psychological effect saved for tactical warfare. When the army moved, so would the Luftwaffe, and General Keitel and General von Brauchitsch said the army was not ready to move. The generals were afraid of the might of the French army. What they did not realize was that if the French had not been morally decrepit as a nation, they would have attacked before this point. The French did not want to fight, and they could not agree among themselves about any plan of defense. The Maginot Line, their defense perimeter against Germany, was extremely strong, but it was a static defense, useful only if the Germans attacked it directly. But what if the Germans came around the north or south end of the line? The French were not thinking about that and, at the moment, neither were the German generals.

Goering wanted action. He was sure that an attenuated war was not in Germany's best interests. But action was not forthcoming.

That winter he got wind of new plans of Hitler's. By this time Hitler was already running the war single-handedly. There was no reason for him to consult Goering about military matters that did not directly involve the air force, and now he did not but, with the Army General Staff, made plans for an invasion of all Scandinavia. When Goering heard of this, he went hastily to the Chancellery to discover what was happening. Hitler confirmed the reports, and for once Goering stood up to the Führer. He had personally promised the Swedes, he said, that they would never be attacked. He had already persuaded them to agree to provide Germany with ores. But what about the movement of troops across Sweden into Norway? asked Hitler. He would fix that, too, said Goering, but Sweden must not be attacked. If this were to happen, Hitler would have to accept his immediate resignation from all posts.

So finally Hitler gave his word to Goering that Sweden would be safe, although he refused to put it in writing. And Goering told the Swedes that they must trust him, that they would not be attacked.

Early in 1940 Hitler devised a plan which would make the French Maginot Line useless. The French had sixty-five divisions and forty-five reserve divisions committed against the Maginot Line. The Germans had only thirty-five divisions there and after the defeat of Poland moved more troops, but still the odds were overwhelming—if the French would fight. The generals stalled, because they did not want to hit that line. Hitler then realized that if he wanted his army to fight, he would have to move in a different direction. Only in the Saarbrücken area were there any engagements. Meanwhile Hitler moved eight armies up to this area.

Hitler grew ever more impatient with the generals. He held that every day lost was a day in which the enemy could strengthen his defenses. He was right in a sense, for across the English Channel the British were building furiously, trying in a few months to put right the defense failures of a quarter of a century. But what Hitler feared was that the powerful French forces would make a lightning thrust at the Ruhr and cut it off. If that happened, Hitler said, the war was lost.

The generals argued. The army was not ready for a real battle, they said. Then get them ready, said Hitler. It would take time, said the generals. There was no time, said Hitler.

Then one day Hitler offered the War Office a plan of his own. The way to attack, he said, was to use the panzers to strike through the enemy line at Sedan, run up the Channel coast at Abbeville and then swing around the rear of the enemy forces, cutting them off.

When the generals saw this plan, they hooted. But one did not. He was General von Manstein, chief of staff to General von Rundstedt's Army Group A. The Hitler plan just happened to agree with one that von Manstein had been urging on von Rundstedt. What must be done was to strike through the neutral lowlands and take positions on the English Channel and the North Sea. From that point, Goering's Luftwaffe could be employed to bring the enemy to their knees. And also the U-boat corps would have bases on the English Channel and the Atlantic shores of France. What an advantage that would be!

The plans were made. And then there was a hitch. A Luftwaffe courier had been sent to army headquarters in Cologne carrying the directive for this new attack. The weather turned bad, and the courier was instructed to go by train. But he got a lift from a friend in the Luftwaffe, and they set out by air. Bad weather caused the pilot to lose his way, and he made an emergency landing in Belgium. The courier tried to destroy the documents but could burn them only partially before he was captured and the documents were turned over to the Belgian police.

When Hitler learned of this, he was furious. He summoned Goering, and Goering was forced to fire General Felmy, the commander of the German air force in the west. Felmy had nothing at all to do with the incident, but Hitler always demanded a scapegoat for any error. And then came the big question: What was to be done? Reluctantly Hitler shelved the plan for the invasion of the Netherlands and Belgium, and the German General Staff breathed a sigh of relief. They would have a little more time.

But not much more time, as it turned out, because Hitler's mind now switched to the Scandinavian countries, where he learned that the British were planning action. The Germans, said Hitler, must get there first.

Hitler did not believe the British would respect the neutrality of Scandinavia—and he was right. The British planned an expeditionary force to go to the assistance of Finland, which was then fighting the Soviet Union in that brief winter war of 1939–40. The expeditionary force, along with French troops, was to go through Scandinavia and occupy the shores of the Baltic, facing the big German bases. The scheme failed on 1 April 1940, when HMS *Cossack,* a British destroyer, steamed into one of the Norwegian fjords to rescue British prisoners held aboard the German auxiliary supply ship *Altmark.* The Norwegian government protested this violation of neutrality, and the Germans seized the excuse to move.

On April 8 the orders were given, and two days later German forces struck Denmark and Norway. Danish resistance was almost nonexistent. How could it be otherwise in a country sharing a common border with Germany, and with very little defense apparatus at all?

But Norway was a different matter. The Germans occupied Bergen, Narvik and Trondheim, but the British came by sea and air and fought, and so did the Norwegians. The Luftwaffe made the difference. At Christiansand, German planes destroyed the forts that guarded the harbor entrance, and troops were landed safely.

At Oslo the navy ran into difficulty, and the heavy cruiser *Blücher* was sunk by the forts. The Germans brought in paratroops, and then the Luftwaffe delivered thousands of reinforcements. Within a few hours the troops had seized all the important airfields, and then the Luftwaffe began operating from Norway, thus effectively interdicting the British attempts to move into the country.

The war in the west remained stagnant that spring until the Norway campaign drew to a close in May.

A British expeditionary force of 400,000 men landed in France. The British then sent Fairey aircraft over the German lines to photograph the West Wall, and the Germans sent reconnaissance planes over the British lines, which extended from Lille to the top of the Maginot Line. The British also sent bombers over Germany, dropping leaflets. German fighters came up to chase the British bombers, but British fighters came up to chase the German fighters, and no one seemed bent on serious warfare. At sea it was quite different. Goering's Luftwaffe and the German navy carried out a fairly effective campaign of harassment of the British trade routes, even then. The aircraft attacked convoys and individual ships and laid mines. The principal value of this air activity was to give experience to the fliers at relatively little risk, and to prove to the British that their Hurricane fighters and Spitfires were indeed superior to the German Messerschmitts and Heinkels.

The first air battle occurred when several German bombers raided the British fleet in the Firth of Forth. One officer and several men aboard a destroyer were killed. The bombers then flew to Edinburgh and Leith but did not bomb.

The Luftwaffe and the U-boat force were creating trouble for the British. The unarmored convoys of the North Sea were the prey of the Luftwaffe, and many ships were sunk.

Mines were also laid by submarines and aircraft, and these caused the sinking of many more merchant ships. For a time the mine was regarded as the No. 1 menace.

But Goering was unable to give his entire attention to the management of the Luftwaffe. Probably he should have turned it over to General Milch, but he could not, for the headiness of the Luftwaffe's success was like fine wine to him.

In that autumn of 1939 and winter of 1940 his real work was in the management of Germany's economy. Hitler, contemplating a war that might last seven years or more, told Goering that he wanted every bit of German economy on a wartime footing. "All enterprises which cannot be furnished with work essential to the war must be shut down," Hitler said.

In November Goering began to order enormous increases in armaments. The production of munitions was to be increased 100 percent in the next two or three years. Already it was happening: car production had decreased from 275,000 in 1938 to 67,000. The army was taking forty percent of the vehicles and would take seventy-five percent the next year. Housing construction came to a halt. Half the consumer goods were to be given to the army.

Goering rushed from one meeting to another, talking about trade, the air force, farming, labor and finance at different meetings within a few hours.

And while he was conferring, his young men of the Luftwaffe were training, training, training. By May 1940 Flying Officer Candidate Heinz Knöke had completed more than two hundred flights and was learning aerobatics in the Focke-Wulf 44.

While he was doing this, his chief, Field Marshal Goering, was cutting the ground out from under the Luftwaffe's fu-

Second Lieutenants Goering and Loerzer at Stenay in the summer of 1916. The plane is an Albatros B-2 with a 100 hp engine.

Lieutenant Goering (right), commander of the Von Richthofen Fighter Squadron, with officers of No. 11 Flight on the western front in August 1918.

German airmen in Berlin during military aircraft trials, 1918. Left to right: Herr Seekatz of the Fokker Aircraft Works; Captain Bruno Loerzer; Lieutenants Goering and Lothar von Richthofen; Second Lieutenants Kirchstein, Krefft, von Malinckrodt and Schubert.

Goering, in Nazi party uniform, gives the "Heil Hitler" salute at the 1934 Nazi party rally.

Hitler in conversation with Goering—an unusually intimate shot. This picture was released after the latter's appointment as field marshal in February 1938.

Visiting Cologne in June 1934.

A speech in the Berlin Sports Palace, announcing the Nazis' Four-Year Plan, October 1936.

With Air Marshal Ernst Udet (right) on a maneuver in Vorpommern, June 1938.

Taking the salute at a parade of the Kondor Legion, newly returned from the civil war in Spain, May 1939.

In civilian clothes. This picture was released in January 1938.

A speech by Hitler to the Reichstag in the Berlin Opera House at the end of the Polish Campaign, October 1939.

On the Channel coast of France during the Battle of Britain, September 1940: Goering studying maps with (from left) the Luftwaffe's General Chief of Staff Hans Jeschonnek, General Bruno Loerzer and Chief-Adjutant Bernd Brauchitsch.

In the uniform of a Reich Marshal. This picture was released in 1940 after his being made architect of Hitler's Four-Year Plan.

Goering, escorted by General Kesselring and Lieutenant-Generals Stumpff and Weise, inspects Luftwaffe units on Luftwaffe Day, 1939.

Addressing a group of German pilots during the Battle of Britain, summer 1940.

On a visit to the Von Richthofen Fighter Squadron on the Channel coast. To Goering's right stands Squadron Commander Wick, December 1940.

With Luftwaffe pilots, January 1941.

Addressing members of the Reichstag.

With Flight Commander Werner Mölders, the Luftwaffe's most decorated fighter ace, in France, 1940.

Berlin, January 1943: Speaking in the memorial hall of the Reich's air ministry on the tenth anniversary of the Nazis' seizing of power.

In the Führer's headquarters ("Werewolf"), Hitler talking to Field Marshal List and Goering, August 1942.

Studying a map on the eastern front, September 1942.

Goering examines an antiaircraft gun on an inspection of troops in 1943.

On a tour of inspection through the destroyed towns of the Rhineland and Ruhr area, Goering talks to two Cologne housewives. "The Marshal expressed his thanks for the heroic behavior of those injured by the bombing." (Original newspaper report.)

On a visit to the eastern front, 1943.

The "press conference" after Goering's capture in May 1945.

In the Grand Hotel at Kitzbühl, Goering talks with Brigadier General Robert J. Stack (right) and Major-General John Dalquist.

Mrs. Hermann Goering sits in the house at Zell am See, Austria, in which she and her husband were hiding from SS troops after having been reportedly condemned to death by Hitler and rescued by soldiers of the Hermann Goering Division. Mrs. Goering suffered a heart attack after her husband was taken prisoner by the Seventh U.S. Army, and was still ill when this picture was taken, in May 1945.

Nuremberg: In this walled court of justice, important Nazis were held awaiting trials—they began in late November 1945.

Conferring with von Ribbentrop (right) behind the back of Hess, in the dock in the Palace of Justice, Nuremberg, December 1945.

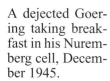

A dejected Goering taking breakfast in his Nuremberg cell, December 1945.

ture. In response to Hitler's demands for "now, now, now," Goering issued an order on February 11. No development work that could not be completed to get the aircraft to the front within a year was to be undertaken, and if it had already been started, it was to be stopped. Thus work stopped on a half-dozen major projects, from jets to long-range bombers. It was a truly fateful decision, and four years later it would be seen to have determined the ultimate fate of the Luftwaffe.

On the surface, everything looked wonderful. The Luftwaffe had started the war with some three thousand serviceable combat aircraft. By March 1940 the air force had nearly four thousand planes.

Hitler had indicated that he was only with difficulty restraining his impatience to move in the west, to defeat France and Britain and get the war over with. Goering not only agreed, he told the Führer that the Luftwaffe was ready to win the war for him.

All that was needed, then, was a decision to move.

14

ANOTHER LIGHTNING WAR

Unlike the British and other Western armies, the German high command had put the control of its paratroop forces under the air force. So it was Hermann Goering's men who started the advance in western Europe that finally ended the *Sitzkrieg* on 10 May 1940.

Two days earlier General Keitel had given the orders that set the whole plan in motion. The key point was the Netherlands. To preserve the international amenities, the Germans had decided to give warning before they attacked, but the warning was to be made in such a way that it would not give the defenders any time to rally.

On the morning of May 9 a diplomatic courier picked up his visa from the Dutch Embassy in Berlin and prepared to take the train to the Netherlands. His mission was to call upon Queen Wilhelmina at the palace—but at six o'clock on the morning of May 10 the queen was unlikely to be up and about and the palace guard scarcely operating. She was to be told, in a message from Hitler, that events of the war had made it imperative that German troops cross the Netherlands in order to get at the enemy on the other side.

The queen was requested to allow the German troops to pass unmolested and was assured that she would not be bothered if she chose to remain in the country. By the time she had read Hitler's note, it was assumed everything would have been done already and she would be facing a fait accompli.

But, as with that other courier a few months earlier, this one also went astray, although in this case it was through no fault of his own. One of Hitler's implacable enemies in Germany was Admiral Wilhelm Canaris, the chief of the military intelligence bureau at the defense high command. He had an agent tip off the Dutch border police that this courier was carrying a secret message. The courier was stopped at the Dutch border and searched, while he protested the violation of his diplomatic immunity (which was valid). Within a matter of hours, the Dutch were flooding their countryside, which would make it difficult for the Germans to pass. The warning did not help a great deal, but it did defeat the Germans in their attempt to effect total surprise.

Even so, the surprise was great next morning just after dawn, when thousands of German paratroops began dropping on Schiphol Airport, the Netherlands main air-transport center. The attack was carried out in the fashion called Cartagena, because it was developed by two German air generals during the Spanish civil war. First bombers attacked the antiaircraft positions and forced the gunners to seek safety. They were followed by dive-bombers and fighters hitting the machine-gun positions, and these were followed by paratroops. So defenders, ducking away from the Stukas with their fearsome noise, raised their heads to find that they were in the hands of German infantrymen.

AIR ASSAULT

In Operation Yellow, the attack on France and the Low Countries, launched on 10 May 1940, Goering's airborne forces had their most spectacular success so far, and the use of tactical air power in support of an army was demonstrated on an unprecedented scale.

—Asher Lee, *Goering: Air Leader*

Seaplanes came in low along the land and landed on the River Maas. Soon their troops had captured the Rotterdam bridges. At the same time Stuka dive-bombers screamed down over Rotterdam and unleashed their bombs. The center of the city was destroyed. The Allies claimed a "foul" and trumpeted the news that thirty thousand people had been killed in the raids. The Germans could not have been more delighted, because the news paralyzed the French and Belgians. In fact, eight hundred people died in these air raids, but a square mile of the city was blown up and burned, and the effect, seen in pictures all over the world, was to frighten civilian populations.

The attack on Rotterdam had been totally unnecessary. The city fathers were in the process of surrendering as the bombers came down, but the word did not get to the Luftwaffe headquarters in time to stop the slaughter. Quite possibly that was intentional, because the Germans had learned the psychological value of the blitz.

On Saturday, May 11, the French newspaper *Paris-soir* headlined the news: "The Germans have invaded Holland, Belgium and Luxembourg." The French cities of Nancy, Lille, Colmar, Lyons, Pontoise and Luxeuil were bombed.

The Dutch surrendered in five days and, seeing what the Nazis could do, the Belgians followed suit.

With these captures and bombings, the Germans then controlled a port from which they could ship troops to Belgium, and two of the best airfields, Waalhaven and Ypenburg, from which the Luftwaffe could operate more easily against Belgium and France.

In the air Goering's Luftwaffe mounted 3,800 aircraft, 1,500 of them bombers and Stukas, and 1,000 fighters, plus observation and transport planes. The Allies had some 2,300 planes, most of them French. The British contingent numbered only about 450 planes on the Continent.

Dr. Goebbels' propaganda campaign indicates that the Luftwaffe had it all its own way in the air, but this was not true. The Luftwaffe casualties were very high: three hundred planes were destroyed and fifty damaged. Despite the Luftwaffe's big buildup by Goebbels, with aid from Goering, it was not nearly so skillful as it seemed to be. For example, on May 10 forty-five Heinkel 111 bombers set out from Landsberg to strike the enemies of the Third Reich. They were all from Edelweiss Air Group, assigned to hit the Dijon area. Most of them lost their way and instead bombed the fighter field at Dôle-Tqvaus. Some did not hit the enemy at all, and three planes bombed the German city of Freiburg im Breisgau, killing fifty-seven people, including twenty-two children. That day the Germans lost eighty-three planes. The next day they lost forty-two planes.

But in other areas the Luftwaffe forces were very skillful indeed. They established beyond all doubt the value of airborne troops in cracking open the enemy's strongest fortified positions.

Several very important bridges in the Albert Canal region were controlled by a superfort called Fort Eben Emael. The bridges lay northwest of the fort. Since 1936 they had been declared safe because the fort was "impregnable," armored, built of reinforced concrete, with access security all around. But the Germans had been studying Fort Eben Emael, with its 1,200-man garrison, and they sent Flying Officer Witzig with Storm Group Granite, which consisted of eighty-four airborne troops. At 4:30 on the morning of May 10, from Cologne and Ostheim, glider troops took off towed by Ju-52 bombers. They came down the Rhine and then turned, and the gliders sailed in through the antiaircraft fire. The assault group hit first, on top of the fortress, and within a matter of minutes they had made the fortress into a tin of peas, spiking the guns, and were opening the tin. They captured nearly 1,200 Belgian soldiers, with a casualty list of five killed and twenty wounded. The fortress garrison lost 200 men.

This German operation was the most spectacular use of airborne troops yet and was soon being used as a lesson in staff schools and training schools in the United States and Britain.

On May 12 the Luftwaffe announced to Goering that it had achieved air superiority and had just about wiped out the French air force. Thereafter the German planes flew mostly in support of the fast-advancing panzer forces. The blitzkrieg on land was on again.

When the news of the German invasion of the Netherlands and Belgium reached the British forces, they were ordered to move. They made a right turn up into Belgium, but the hinge on which the British army moved at the edge of the Maginot Line was precisely where General Heinz Guderian's panzers struck in their break through the Ardennes Forest into the Sedan. The Germans began pouring into France, swept straight across to the Channel ports and by May 26 occupied Cologne. The British army was cut off.

On May 13 the Germans crossed the Meuse. The Luftwaffe provided continual close support. The plan worked like clockwork, and in two days most forces were across. They had a run for Abbeville. On the shore the Allied air forces tried to destroy the German bridges across the Meuse, but the Germans fought them off in the air and on the ground. On May 15 the Allies threw all the air strength they could muster against the Meuse bridges but failed to destroy them. On May 17 the German fighters established their operations base at Charleville, west of the Meuse, and from there the Luftwaffe carried out murderous attacks on the French Channel coast.

The Germans were moving very fast—so fast that General von Rundstedt became nervous. He was not quite sure where all his troops were. In the third week of May, as the British were making their way laboriously to the coast near Dunkirk, it seemed that the Germans could drive them into the sea, but von Rundstedt was worried. So he stopped the drive on Hitler's orders. He did not wish to be trapped. He believed that the enemy was on the ropes and that the delay of a few days, while the support forces came up with supplies and fuel, would not make much difference in the destruction of the enemy.

Now the Stukas came into action again. They were used very intelligently, to hit concentrations. A gun battery or a small stand of troops would be struck by a flight of Stukas and decimated.

As one British air expert put it, the roads of France were cleared by the Germans' machine-gunning, not by heavy bombing. Whether the people on the roads were retreating troops or refugees, they were shot down and the road was clear for the advance of the German tanks and armored cars and motorized infantry. The French air force was demoralized and decimated. The British Expeditionary Air Force was too small to do much to stop the German tide. Ultimately the British squadrons left their planes and sought safety on the roads.

The movement was so swift that Cadet Knöke lamented the fact that the war would be over before he had a chance to get into action. As the Stukas roared down on France, he was learning to fly half a dozen different sorts of aircraft.

Then, on May 25, a euphoric Hermann Goering told Adolf Hitler that he need not worry about the coming operations against Britain, because he was now convinced that the Luftwaffe could defeat Britain single-handedly and wipe up the Dunkirk beaches with them.

So the drive was not started again. This failure gave the British a chance to entrench, hold fortified positions and begin an orderly withdrawal by small boats from the Dunkirk coast.

On May 26 the British evacuation began. For the next nine days the skies above France were filled with air battles. The Germans came from Germany with their bombers, to try to knock out the British evacuation. But British fighters came from Britain to do battle with the bombers and the German fighters that arose from the French fields, and the conflict raged during the daylight hours.

By June 3 the RAF had lost 177 aircraft, but the Germans had lost 240, and that meant that by the end of the French campaign they had lost 1,400 aircraft, about thirty percent of their total.

Although at the operational level these losses were considered excessive and worrisome, Goering did not have much time to spend worrying about them. As an old fighter pilot, he felt that this was the winnowing-out period, where the least fit were the first to go. He had no concern about the future, he said.

On the day the Dunkirk evacuation ended, Goering came up to a railway tunnel near the Channel, in his armored train, and called a conference of his Luftwaffe commanders.

Generals Milch, Kesselring and Jeschonnek, commander of the western air forces, came to the meeting. Goering asked a few questions, but mostly he talked about what he wanted to do in the future. If the commanders agreed, he said, he was going to propose to the Führer that Germany make an almost immediate assault on Britain. He was so full of confidence over the storming of the Belgian forts that he said he believed a few army divisions with some paratroop training could reinforce the Luftwaffe's one parachute division. Then he would put together another five divisions of airborne troops in reserve. He told his generals that they were to bring the Luftwaffe to a constant state of readiness, for an attack at any moment.

Goering went to Hitler and made the proposal, but Hitler was not much interested at the moment. He saw that he had defeated France. He expected the British now to become much more malleable. He put Goering off.

Later Hitler suggested that the British could be brought around by Germany's guaranteeing their empire, if they would only acknowledge Germany's new Continental empire. Hitler said he wanted to make peace with Britain. But in London Winston Churchill had replaced Neville Chamberlain as prime minister, and Churchill vowed that Britain would fight to the bitter end, until Hitler was defeated and Europe freed.

CHURCHILL DEFIANT

I have nothing to offer but blood, tears, toil and sweat.
—Churchill to Parliament in 1940

We shall go on to the end—; Whatever the cost may be we shall fight on the beaches, we shall fight on the landing grounds, we shall fight on the fields and in the streets, we shall fight in the hills; we shall never surrender.
—Churchill to Parliament in 1940

Goering was convinced (without very good reason) that, if the Luftwaffe struck now and was supported by more paratroops and then sea landings, Britain could be defeated. But there were holes in the argument. First, paratroops are not made overnight by the assignment of divisions. Training is arduous and dangerous, and the losses are high. And as for the follow-up, Germany had virtually no landing craft with which it could stage an amphibious invasion. In the summer of 1940 it simply could not have been done.

And so Hermann Goering gave up his scheme, which pleased the Luftwaffe generals for the most part, since they knew better than Goering how unready they were for a major offensive of that sort. He went off to Compiègne Forest with Hitler, dressed in his field marshal's uniform, and shared in the triumph—the erasure of the shame of Versailles.

The Germans then went to Paris to exult in their victory. All this was now theirs. Hermann Goering took this dictum literally. He began visiting France's museums, with an eye to acquiring the Old Masters of Europe. During his marriage to

---

SWEET REVENGE

Here on the 11th of November, 1918, the criminal pride of
the German Empire succumbed, defeated by thc free peoples which it tried to enslave.

—Inscription on railway coach at Forest of Campiègne

It was very satisfying to read that, as the second leader of
a newly victorious Germany, to enjoy the warmth of the
June sunshine, and to know that the shame of defeat had
been wiped out.

—Ewan Butler and Gordon Young,
The Life and Death of Hermann Goering

Carin, he had learned much from her about art. Since that
time he had become a collector and had often requisitioned
treasures from the German museums for his own collection.
Now he would embark on a gigantic campaign of appropriation of the masterpieces of Europe that appealed to him.

So for a while, Goering dallied among the treasures, while
General Milch and the others set to work to prepare for the
campaign that Goering had laid out. They must rebuild the
Luftwaffe in a hurry. They must redeploy their forces onto
permanent French bases for an attack on Britain. The task
was not made easier by Hitler's belief that all this would not
be necessary. All the British needed, he said, was a little
talking around to realize that Germany was no threat to the
British Empire.

On July 19 Hitler held a victory meeting of the Reichstag
and used this podium for an appeal to Britain to stop the
war. He said that Britain could have peace any time it

wanted it. "I consider myself in a position to make this appeal since I am not the vanquished begging favors, but the victor, speaking in the name of reason. I can see no reason why this war should go on."

No, Hitler could not. But across the Channel, Winston Churchill could see every reason for the war to go on. He did not believe Hitler or his protestations of peace loving. He did not believe that the British Empire was safe as long as the Nazis roamed the world.

Secure in his belief that the war was almost ended, Hitler turned to rewarding the faithful. Goering became the Reich Marshal of the Greater German Reich, the highest military officer in the land.

HONORED BY HITLER

As a reward for his mighty contribution to victory, I hereby appoint the creator of the Luftwaffe to the rank of Reich Marshal of the Greater German Reich, and award him the Cross of the Iron Cross.

—Hitler

Generals Milch, Kesselring and Sperrle of the Luftwaffe were all promoted to the rank of field marshal. The Luftwaffe had come into its own within the German military establishment.

Within an hour of Hitler's appeal, the answer came on the British Broadcasting Corporation's Germany beam. The answer was no.

That night the German generals and field marshals celebrated, and Goering and his party grew tipsy. Then came dawn, and the hangover, the realization that Britain was not going to give up and that, unless there was some way of stopping British resistance, the quick victory over France did not mean that the war would be short. So what was Goering going to do now?

15

THE BATTLE OF BRITAIN

On 18 June 1940 Winston Churchill told the House of Commons that they must expect the Battle of Britain to begin momentarily, that it was going to be an intensive battle and that on the outcome depended the fate of nations.

Hitler's original plans for empire had turned to the east, not the west. Had Britain and France acceded to the conquest of Poland, they would have been safe for a time—until the megalomania grew greater. But when they refused, Hitler was angry and set about their destruction.

As seen, the destruction of a France riddled with corruption and doubt was not a great task. As nations usually begin a war with the weapons of the past, so had France. Her generals had learned well from World War I and knew a great deal about trench warfare, but the Germans, forbidden the normal military thinking for fifteen years under the Versailles treaty, had responded by improvising and had developed the spearhead warfare of tanks and air force, and France, with all her divisions, found herself enveloped and defeated in just over a month.

What then? After Hitler had celebrated his victory and shipped the old railway carriage that had seen two major surrenders in less than a quarter of a century back to Berlin as a curiosity, he then had to consider what to do about Britain.

He—and Goering and the Wehrmacht—had missed their chance to cripple Britain's military strength at Dunkirk. By stopping the lightning thrust while they still had the advantage, the Germans had let the British get away with most of their men and some of their equipment. Hitler's ploy—the grandiose gesture of again offering the British peace—had failed miserably, and now Hitler had either to stop, digest his victory and watch the enemy grow ever more powerful or to take some action. So swiftly had the victory over France come, and so unexpected was the British determination to continue to fight on alone against Germany, that the masters of the Third Reich were not quite sure what to do.

General Jodl, the No. 2 man of the forces' high command, had been ordered to come up with a plan. He had explored the options: Germany could attack Britain either peripherally or directly. If she attacked peripherally, it meant moving in the Mediterranean and on the sea approaches to Britain. Being an island, Britain was dependent on the sea for her existence, and the submarines and the Luftwaffe could control the sea.

This argument appealed greatly to Goering and to Admiral Dönitz, the commander of the German U-boat force. If Hitler would give him three hundred submarines, Dönitz had said several years before the war, he could put Britain out of action in six months. But Hitler had not listened then and he scarcely listened now.

The second method of dealing with Britain would be the direct attack. This would involve first an offensive by sea and air against British shipping, as Dönitz and Goering wanted, then terror attacks from the air against Britain's cities, to frighten the population and prepare them for the third step, the actual invasion of the islands, Operation Sea Lion.

When he had considered the options, Hitler decided on the three-pronged attack against Britain directly.

HITLER VS. ENGLAND

On July 16, Hitler issued his Directive No. 16: "Since England, in spite of her hopeless military situation, shows no sign of coming to an understanding, I have decided to prepare a landing operation and if necessary carry it out." The aim of the operation, baptized "Sea Lion" was "to eliminate the English homeland as a base for the prosecution of the war against Germany."

He did not know, and did not care, that the German navy did not have the landing craft to make an assault on Britain or that the German navy, having built the wrong sort of ships and employed them badly in the opening days of the war, did not have the surface navy to protect the amphibious landings.

Meanwhile, urged on by Goering, the action Hitler chose to take was the blasting of Britain from the air. During the Spanish civil war an Italian general named Douhet had developed a theory of total air warfare. He was not the only one. In America Alexander de Seversky was flying high with a theory called "Victory Through Air Power." Goering was convinced that his Luftwaffe alone could bring Britain down and that an invasion was unnecessary. General Alfred Jodl, the No. 2 man of the high command staff, agreed with Goering. Once the air-and-sea campaign had succeeded, they both said, the landings would be easy and the British would be ready for occupation.

Hitler moved his scene of operations to Tannenberg, in the Black Forest, west of Freudenstadt, and here he expected to oversee the conquest of Great Britain.

Goering had set up his military headquarters in Paris, where he could eat at Fouquet's, Le Tour d'Argent and Maxim's and commune with the art world and select the Old Masters he would cart off to Carinhall.

PATRON OF THE ARTS

I have now obtained by means of purchase, presents, bequests, and barter perhaps the greatest private collection in Germany at least, if not in Europe.

—In Goering's letter to Alfred Rosenberg

Allied experts placed the figure at 180 million dollars— Goering's magnificent art collection of 1,300 or more paintings.

—Eugene Davidson, *The Trial of the Germans*

He commuted by armored train to be with his generals and usually parked the train while in the field, on a siding near Calais, close to a tunnel into which it could be run in case of British air attack.

The train, named *Asia,* was a tribute to his love of luxury. It consisted of some ordinary coaches, a baggage coach that carried cars, an open gondola carriage mounted with antiaircraft guns, and Goering's special carriage, with two sleeping compartments, a small workroom and a luxurious bathroom. Then came another carriage, with lounge seats and a living room that had a cinema projector; a third carriage, with a conference room and working area; and a fourth carriage, which had a fine kitchen and dining area. Goering could entertain here almost as royally as at Carinhall.

RICH DINING

The food was of an elegant kind: strawberries might be flown in from Italy by the accompanying courier planes, rolls and cakes could be baked in ovens of the train, and an ordinary lunch often included lobster and caviar as well as Italian fruit.

—Eugene Davidson, *The Trial of the Germans*

On June 30 he signed the orders for the air war against Britain.

FALSE CONFIDENCE

For the first time in modern history the people of England are now to feel the full and direct impact of war on their own soil. Their morale is expected to deteriorate in consequence.

—Goering

First the Luftwaffe would attack the British fighter airfields, bomber fields, support groups and aircraft plants. Once these were diminished, it would be possible to have free range across Britain, attacking ports and ships in the harbor, convoys along the shore, and British industry. But the first target, as Goering made quite clear, was the Royal Air Force and its supply chain, and that must be eliminated before the other targets could be addressed.

In July, the Germans began some tentative probing of British air defenses while they hurriedly made plans for the major air assault. Several major problems had to be overcome. The heavy losses of the French campaign meant that planes had to be secured from somewhere, and "somewhere" turned out to be the training command, which was stripped to the bone of aircraft and superior pilots. At the same time the argument that no aircraft that could not be put on the line within a year was to be given further testing kept the Luftwaffe from developing new weapons.

When that announcement was made by Goering, Ernst Udet threw up his hands in despair. "The war is finished," he said, for he knew that, without development of new weapons—and long-range bombers at that—Germany could never win the air war. But by this time Udet had fallen out of favor, even though he was made an air-force general in July. Several of his designs had not yet matured, and Hitler was becoming ever more demanding that every experiment be immediately successful. Therefore the Luftwaffe development campaign came to a halt.

In the fruit of their victory over France, and their ambitions against Britain, lay the seeds of the destruction of the Luftwaffe, but no one recognized this fact. The Luftwaffe chief of staff, Hans Jeschonnek, was a young man, still in his early forties, with a sarcastic air that infuriated his equals and terrorized his subordinates. He seemed supremely confident of victory in the coming battle against Britain.

At a meeting aboard his train, Goering asked Jeschonnek if he thought the attacks would be successful.

"I certainly think so," said the confident young chief of staff.

Goering asked him how long he thought it would take to knock Britain out of the war.

"I count on only six weeks more," said Jeschonnek.

"I doubt that," said Goering, who knew the British. "You know, a German would fight on, even if Berlin would be totally destroyed, and the Englishman is not going to be any easier than the German. No, he will fight on, if London is destroyed."

The British, he said, were not like the French, who, when Paris was occupied, simply gave up the struggle.

The whole Luftwaffe establishment was, in fact, riding on a cloud in July 1940. Jeschonnek had just been promoted to general, as had Udet and others. The halls of Germany were ringing with the praise of the invincible Luftwaffe and its magnificent Stuka bombers, even though the British at Dunkirk had discovered that the Stuka was remarkably easy to shoot down because it was slow and because the rear gunner's weapon would not traverse past the midpoint of the aircraft. But the Stuka myth persisted.

So the generals met, and they considered the problem. Which element should have priority? Should they concentrate, as Admiral Dönitz had been urging, on the blockade of Britain, to starve the enemy out? Should they mass their air strength to destroy the British air force, and then let the German army do the rest?

They received no guidance from Hitler, whose eye was already turned east, in his mania that he must destroy Communism before Communism destroyed him. So Goering and his generals were left to figure out the approach to the war against Britain. And if Goering had been a strategic genius, which he was not, still his duties elsewhere in the Reich made it impossible for him to give full consideration to the problems of the Luftwaffe. His major idea had already been discarded by Hitler: to launch an immediate aerial battle in June and then to use ordinary infantry as paratroops and capture Britain before she could recover from the debacle on the Continent.

The first step in the Battle of Britain was a series of attacks, launched in June and July, against British shipping and port facilities. Those attacks on Britain had come from the Calais area. The German air forces stationed in Norway did not have the range to hit Britain, and since the bombers needed two or three escorts, because they were very vulnerable, using them was much too expensive for Goering. So the Calais air fleet was called on for the opening parts of the job.

Goering's faith in the Stuka was such that he ordered that that machine be the central core of the attack, and so masses of dive-bombers with fighter escorts were sent out to attack British shipping in the English Channel. The results were disastrous. Back on their home territory the British fighter pilots had the range to launch and sustain attacks. Some fighters engaged the German fighter planes, others picked off the Stukas.

When that campaign failed, the Luftwaffe turned to the level bombers, the Heinkels and the Dorniers. But here the problem of lack of proper armament showed itself. The Heinkels and Dorniers were stair-stepped in altitude, sandwiched with fighters, up to thirty thousand feet. And here the problem was created by the inadequacy of the German air-intelligence system. In a study made that summer, Luftwaffe intelligence told Goering that the Spitfire and the Hurricane were underpowered and could not fight at high altitude. Nor did the Germans recognize the efficacy of the British radar-controlled air-defense system, because at that point they did not understand it. Therefore, when the flights of Heinkels and Dorniers came over at medium to high altitude, they, too, were shot down in large numbers.

DOG FIGHT

I moved out to the left and it was then that I saw, unmistakable, on the side of the fuselage, the black German cross. The plane was a Dornier 17.—Coming in from their left and slightly above, still concealed from the searchlights, I held on until the last moment, then pressed the firing button. A short burst—thirty rounds from each gun—and it was over. The effect of the De Wilde was terrible; the Dornier's controls were hit, its incendiaries set on fire.—Down went the Dornier again in a steep spiral, to crash with its load of bombs."

—Peter Townsend, *The Odds Against Us*

The Luftwaffe continued its planning for the late-summer assault. It would take only four days to knock out British air defenses, Goering was told. Then would come four weeks of mopping up, at the end of which there would be nothing left of the RAF or the British aircraft industry.

And so, as the Luftwaffe suffered serious attrition in the prebattle stage, the plans continued with very little recognition of reality. The Luftwaffe would win air superiority immediately by attack on the RAF and industry. Next the Luftwaffe would attack and cripple the British fleet, then the British ports would be destroyed, and finally the terror bombing of the cities would finish the task.

The preliminary stage rolled into high gear on July 1, and

the statistics looked very favorable to the Germans. Their 2nd and 3rd Air Fleets, which would be involved, boasted 1,100 medium bombers, nearly 320 dive-bombers and 800 single-engine fighters.

The strategy was a gift to the British. It let them try out some new techniques, and it gave them time to build more fighters and to work the bugs out of the radar system of warning and control.

The German forces involved were massed along the air front from Brussels to Paris and concentrated on the southeast sector of England. General Kesselring's 2nd Air Fleet had its headquarters southwest of Brussels. General Sperrle's 3rd Air Fleet's headquarters was just southeast of Paris. The bombers were the Heinkels, Dorniers and Junkers 52s. The fighters were the Me-109s and Me-110s. The Stukas, which started with such a roar, were quickly relegated to a secondary position when their losses grew high.

Against this force at the beginning of August the British had over 700 Spitfire and Hurricane fighters and that greater advantage, radar control and warning systems. So the forces were preparing to join battle.

German losses mounted; so did the problems. Luftwaffe headquarters was dismayed to see that fighter-aircraft production, instead of rising, had been falling, because of the cutbacks in research and development and through bad planning. Only 375 fighters were being produced each month in the German factories. And then, even before the major offensive was launched, it became apparent that the dauntless Stuka was dauntless no more. In the attacks on shipping, where Goering had ordered the use of Stukas because of their pinpoint bombing, the dive-bombers were falling like flies to the British fighters.

As August began, so did the foul weather of a strange

summer. The spring, when the Germans had been rolling up victory after victory, had been calm and sunny, but now the clouds came in, and the Channel became a murky, squally battlefield.

On August 1 Hitler issued Order No. 17, regarding the war against Britain. It involved the coordination of land, air and sea forces. Dönitz's submarines were now to sink passenger ships on sight, without warning, and to increase the war at sea against the western approaches to Britain. "Eagle Day," set for August 13, was the day on which Goering's Luftwaffe would overwhelm the British, the beginning of the four-day period in which they would knock out the Spitfires and the Hurricanes.

For the coming battle, a line was drawn from Bristol to Cambridge. This would be the battle zone. The latest air-intelligence estimates seemed very promising. The RAF should be able to secure reinforcement of only 180 fighters a month, and this number could drop as soon as the factories were bombed.

But what Goering did not know was that his own Luftwaffe had suffered seriously. Between May 10 and July 31 it had lost 2,600 aircraft, and the fighter force was down to seventy percent of its strength before the attack on France. Further, the losses had barely been made up by production, and production was falling.

Goering was also badly served by his air-intelligence chief, Josef Schmid, who had just told him, "The Luftwaffe is vastly superior to the RAF as regards strength, equipment, training, command and location of bases." However, British fighter production was not 180 per month, but nearly 500 per month.

On Monday, August 12, Luftwaffe Stukas and Messerschmitt 110 fighters set out to bomb the British radar stations at Dunkirk, Pevensey, Rye, Dover and Ventnor. They did a good job, knocking out the sending aerials of several stations. So the stage was set for what the Germans called *Adlertag*—Eagle Day.

Reich Marshal Goering was very confident. He now had 1,300 bombers, 700 fighters and 260 Stukas against the British 700 fighters and 500 bombers. The war should be over in a few days.

The day began at 7:00 A.M. A stream of bombers and fighters set out from the French and Belgian fields; in all, 1,000 fighters and 485 bombers were employed, and the Germans lost only 34 planes.

The attacks continued. On Wednesday they sent 700 planes, and 45 were shot down. The British radar was working again, and it was very effective in rallying the defending fighters to the right places at the right times. "Two passes, two planes" was the motto. The British were well organized, and they knew precisely what they had to do. The Germans were not so well organized, and they did not have radar. It made all the difference, for the British fighters could be vectored out swiftly to any area threatened, and so many of the German planes never reached the shores of Britain at all but were shot down over the North Sea or in the Channel.

On Thursday, August 15, the Germans sent 2,100 missions over southern England and lost 57 planes. On Friday the 16th they sent out 1,720 planes. Fighter Command met them again, and while the British lost 21 planes, the Germans lost 45.

The Germans then attacked the British airfields at Kenley and Tangmere, as well as Croydon, West Malling, Manston and Biggin Hill, and the results were even worse for Goering's boys: they lost 71 planes to the RAF's 27. This ended the first phase of the Air Strike Against England.

Monday, August 19, was the opening of the second phase of the air war. Airfields and aircraft factories in southern England were the targets. By this time the British radar was not only totally repaired, it had been improved, and the Germans lost more planes. On August 24 they sent their first bombing raid against London in very bad weather. They were heading for the inner city, and they hit St. Giles and

INTO THE AIR

At last it came. "Off you go!" called the Kenley controller, and we were racing forward with the bellow of our combined 12,000 horsepower.

Bombs were already falling toward Croydon. Just off the ground, my engine faltered, then picked up again. Blast had hit it like a punch in the wind. Turning in the cockpit, I saw the rest of the squadron emerging from a vast eruption of smoke and debris. Thank God, they too had survived the blast. I looked up. Thousands of feet above, the 110s were wheeling in the blue, Me-109s swarming above.—"Get the 110s but watch out for the 109s!" . . .

A Me-110 was firing at me; I could see in the corner of my eye the flashing of its two 20mm cannons and four machine guns. The salvo blasted my poor Hurricane, holing the central fuel tank, starring the bulletproof windscreen, and hitting me with a thump in the left foot. The engine was dead;—so over the side I went. Once again my parachute saved me. Hanging on the end of it, I watched my Hurricane dive headlong into the trees and blow up.

—Pilot Peter Townsend of the Royal Air Force

Cripplegate. Nine people were killed. They also tried to attack targets in Bristol, Liverpool and Birmingham.

In all this, the Germans made woeful miscalculations. By August 20, the German intelligence men calculated that the British had lost 644 planes; actually the RAF had lost only 103. One field had been temporarily put out of action, but the Germans believed they had knocked out eleven fields.

On the night of September 5, sixty-eight planes from Air Groups 2, 3, 26 and 53 set out on what was intended to be the terrorization of British cities. They carried sixty tons of bombs and were heading for the docks and the aircraft plants. This, said Goering, was the start of the "strategic bombing" campaign against Britain. But he did not have the reserves, or the big planes, to carry out a real strategic bombing campaign, although he did not know it. Still the Germans persisted. On September 7, they sent three hundred bombers and seven hundred fighters against the east and west sectors of London. Marshal Goering himself saw them off, accompanying the flights as far as Cape Gris-Nez.

This, said he, would be the beginning of the third phase of the air war against Britain which would last until October 5. How dates had changed! What had happened to the four days that were supposed to knock the RAF out of the war? The Luftwaffe had failed miserably, and now the results of that failure were becoming known throughout the command. And on this night the losses were enormous: of 250 planes sent over, only 103 bombed. Of course, this was not admitted. The bluff continued.

Yet with all the manipulation of figures, by mid-September it was clear that the Luftwaffe was virtually exhausted. Goering had lost his nephew Peter, and many of the best-trained and most skillful pilots were gone. Something had to be done.

On September 15, the Germans came again, and this time they lost a quarter of their bombers. The losses were too great. A change had to be made, so Goering switched from day to night bombing. On Monday, September 30, it began. Again, the effects were not positive. At the end of October Goering totaled it up. In reality the British had lost 915 planes by that time, while German loss was 1,733. And while British aircraft production was increasing, German aircraft production was still staggering, because of the poor planning of the previous two years and the inability of the Germans to improvise, as did their enemy.

In mid-September, Hitler instructed Goering to make one final attempt to end the war through air power alone, by heavy night bombing of the cities, airfields and industry. But it failed. The damage to Britain's cities was heavy.

CITY ON FIRE

—Heinkels loaded with incendiaries only, accomplished its mission—. They laid down a carpet of fire—. Visible from afar, despite the broken cloud drifting over London—. The burning city kindled into a huge brazier.—It looked as if the whole city was on fire and the sky above as well.

—Ray Callow, a viewer

By the end of October, 15,000 civilians had been killed, 21,000 wounded. In 333 bombing attacks, the Germans had dropped tons of fire bombs and explosives, but they had lost hundreds more planes, while the British losses were about a quarter of the German. So another ploy had failed.

16

THE BLITZ

In August 1940, Corporal Heinz Knöke of the Luftwaffe was posted to the fighter school in Werneuchen and assigned to instructor Flight Sergeant Kuhl, who had served in Poland and France. The commandant of the school was Colonel Count Huwald, who had been one of Goering's pilots in the Richthofen Air Group in World War I. The chief instructor was Major von Kornatzky, who until recently had been Goering's personal adjutant. The training of the fighter pilots then was improving a little, but not so much could be said of transport and bomber pilots.

By September Pilot Knöke had hoped to be posted to a combat unit, but the training program was languishing from lack of funds, lack of planes and lack of decent flying weather.

Training was now in the Me-109, a very difficult plane to fly. It cost several lives among the class before the others mastered the tricky controls and uncertain approach to landing that was inherent in the aircraft.

Although Hitler now had reservations about the efficacy of the Luftwaffe, which would grow quickly into doubts, Reich

Marshal Goering was at the apogee of his career. Carinhall, the private estate of 100,000 acres with only his house and a few villages inside, was now his playground, and there he invited the chosen few to hunt stags and dine amid the trophies on the walls and the bearskin rugs and silver and gold and crystal of his table. He had brought the finest of wines and liqueurs from defeated France. The feasting and the atmosphere were such that one of his Italian guests compared Goering to one of the Borgias, a family more notable in Italy for its excesses in luxury than for its poisonous women.

In the autumn of 1940, just as the bombing of London turned into the terror campaign ordered by Hitler, Goering invited fighter ace Adolf Galland to another hunting lodge on Rominten Heath, and there the essentially conservative Galland had an unusual view of his swashbuckling commander. Goering greeted him wearing a green suede hunting jacket, jackboots and a silk shirt with puffed sleeves reminiscent of the seventeenth century. A huge hunting knife was jammed in his belt, and he wore a little hat adorned with a long pheasant feather.

While Galland was there, the terror campaign began, on September 7, with the strike of 1,300 bombers and fighters aiming at the Woolwich Arsenal. They hit gasworks, which flamed beautifully if tragically, power stations and miles and miles of docks. In two nights a thousand people were killed and three thousand wounded.

Night after night the German bombers dropped their bombs. On September 15, the Luftwaffe staged a big daylight raid involving two hundred bombers and six hundred fighters. Most of the bombers were turned away without hitting their targets, for the British radar system was working admirably and the British fighters appeared where they were needed. The Germans counted their losses after this raid: 150 planes destroyed and more than a hundred badly damaged. The British had lost about twenty-five planes. This sort of ratio was disastrous, and Goering was very much upset by it. He was losing the cream of his Luftwaffe.

Between September 7 and October 5 the Germans had made thirty-eight attacks and had lost 883 planes. The 2nd and 3rd Air Fleets had been decimated.

All gone were the strictures laid down by Goering in the beginning that the Luftwaffe should engage in nothing but pinpoint bombing. Now the fliers had turned to area bombing. Terror and destruction of life and property were the aim of the Dark Night Attack program. It was already apparent to Hitler, though less so to Goering, that the Luftwaffe had failed completely in its aim of destroying the British will to fight.

LOSING MOMENTUM

Hitler had ordered "crush" the RAF, it was evident that the RAF was so far uncrushable. Fighter Command, though badly diminished, was still fighting back. Bomber Command was attacking Berlin and lashing out nightly against the German invasion fleet—to the discomfort of the Kriegsmarine which Hitler was counting on to transport his invasion troops to England's shores.

—Peter Townsend, *The Odds Against Us*

Operation Sea Lion, the invasion of Britain, was postponed indefinitely.

From this point on, Goering would not again have the full

confidence of Hitler as an aeronautical expert. More and more the Führer would take into his own hands the management of the air war. This did not seem to affect Goering's immediate relationship with Hitler; the erosion was slow and gradual. Goering was still the economic master of the Third Reich, and Hitler still depended on him in that capacity, and as a sounding board for his strategic concepts.

On October 22 came a new development. The German planes attacking Britain were joined by 150 Italian fighters and bombers, stationed at the Epinette airfield near Brussels. But with the month that strategy had changed again. The Germans now wanted to try to knock out the British aircraft industry, hoping thus to soften up the defenses, so on the night of November 14, 450 German bombers hit the center of the British aircraft engine works at Coventry. They came in from various directions, assembled at a point 250 miles from the city and then regrouped.

The attack was successful; only two bombers were lost to antiaircraft fire because of the nature of the approach, and they dropped 503 tons of high explosive and 880 fire-bomb clusters. The result was serious destruction of the city and the industry, 554 people killed and 865 seriously injured.

Next the Germans turned their attention to Birmingham, and on the night of November 19 made several raids. But the bombing did not knock out British industry as Goering had hoped.

And then came an event that changed the whole nature of the air war against Britain.

Since the spring of 1940 the British had invaded German airspace many times, to observe military movements and to drop propaganda leaflets.

HITLER'S WAR

The war which Hitler started will go on—as long as Hitler does. . . .

—Peter Townsend, *The Odds Against Us*

They had bombed German shipping and German warships in Norway. They had established a night-bombing system. But the first big raid was conducted by thirty Wellington and twelve Whitley bombers of the 3rd and 4th Groups of RAF Bomber Command on Berlin. They dropped fifty tons of high-explosive bombs, killing twenty-five people and wounding fifty, and returned with the loss of only two planes.

The bombing of Berlin infuriated Hitler, because it was embarrassing, and it caused him to demand of Goering the immediate concentration of bombardment against British cities.

"TOTAL DESTRUCTION"

I want fire everywhere. Thousands of them! Then they'll unite in one gigantic area conflagration. Goering has the right idea. Explosive bombs don't work, but it can be done with incendiary bombs—total destruction of London!

—Adolf Hitler, 1940

Thus the factories were now spared, and the civil population of Britain was brought under fire. The war had been extended to the point at which it could be said there were no more noncombatants in Britain. With the establishment of this new German bombing policy, war became officially a "total war," and the last vestiges of the old gentlemanly ways now disappeared.

NO HOLDS BARRED

This moment is a historic one. As a result of the provocative British attacks on Berlin on recent nights the Führer has decided to order a mighty blow to be struck in revenge against the capital of the British Empire. I personally have assumed the leadership of this attack and today I have heard above me the roaring of the victorious German squadrons.

—Goering

From the autumn of 1940, it was kill or be killed, with no quarter. The policy of "unconditional surrender" (which was neither very wise nor very effective) stemmed largely from this involvement of the civil population.

Goering did not like the prospects. He had thought he could win the Battle of Britain, if not by knocking out the Royal Air Force, then by destroying British industry. But now he was forced to expend the Luftwaffe's efforts in blowing up buildings in big cities and killing women and children to appease the Führer's wrath. He began to believe that he could not win the Battle of Britain on these terms.

It was proved to be true. In October 1940 German planes dropped 9,000 tons of bombs. The next month the tonnage dropped to 6,500 tons. By February 1941 it was down to

1,100 tons. Nor were the bombs going where Hitler wanted them, into the heart of the big cities. The Luftwaffe commanders bridled at the terror campaign, and unless a mission was specifically ordered for a specific place, they diverted the bombers to military targets.

By the spring of 1941 even Hitler had lost interest in the blitz. His mind had turned toward the Soviet Union, and he was counseling the saving of planes to put against the Red Army when he launched his invasion that summer.

And in the spring of 1941, the holes began to appear in the fabric of Goering's coat as economics leader of Germany. Aircraft production fell to just about half the planned norm. In January only 650 planes of all types were produced. This drop was not due entirely to bad planning by Goering and his people: Hitler kept interfering. In the autumn of 1940 he had rescinded the order giving the Luftwaffe priority for materials and turned the attention to the army, building up for the Soviet adventure. There just was not enough raw material to go around.

The shock to Goering came at the end of 1940, when Hitler issued Directive No. 21, for Operation Barbarossa, the preemptive strike on the Soviet Union.

GRAND EXPECTATIONS

There are two possibilities for me: To win through with all my plans, or to fail. If I win, I shall be one of the greatest men in history. If I fail, I shall be condemned, despised, and damned.

—Hitler

Despite the failure of the Luftwaffe to force Britain's capitulation, Goering had not given up hope of making Britain an ally instead of an enemy. He proposed to send a strong force into the Mediterranean, defeat the British there and then force them to join Germany in the war against the Soviet Union. At first Hitler seemed to favor this plan, but as the spring of 1941 came around, he turned against it. He was convinced that Stalin was preparing to attack Germany, and this delusion caused him to forget that Germany's defeat in 1918 had been caused largely by the difficulties of fighting a two-front war.

Goering was very much aware of this, and the thought horrified him. He wanted to use fifteen divisions to defeat the British in the Mediterranean, but Hitler said he had no divisions to waste thus and ordered Goering to stop talking about the Mediterranean. Goering had been saying that he had the most powerful air force in the world, Hitler sneered. Now let him prove it by winning in the Soviet Union.

Goering went back to Carinhall and called for Milch and Jeschonnek. Milch believed Goering backed the Führer's ideas, and was privately horrified. He predicted that the Germans would be bogged down in the Soviet Union for years. Jeschonnek was delighted with the idea of a "proper war" in which the Luftwaffe would be used to support troops, not to bomb civilians or factories.

Goering's hopes for a defeat of Britain in the south seemed to be about to come true, given a little aid from Germany's gallant Italian ally. Mussolini had entered the war against Britain in the summer of 1940, but the Italians had not done much until they decided to attack Greece. They did attack, and the war went very well for a few weeks. But in the autumn of 1940, when Goering was depressed by Luftwaffe failures against Britain, he also had other bad news. The

Italians fighting in the mountains of Greece were taking a beating. Then came the Italian naval disaster at Taranto, when British carrier planes smashed the fleet, and finally the collapse of Italian forces fighting the British in Libya. In January the British destroyed a whole Italian army and took 100,000 prisoners.

So in spite of Hitler's plans for Operation Barbarossa, he now had to move into the Mediterranean and extricate the Italians from the difficulty they had caused. The first move was to make Goering send the 10th Flying Corps to Sicily. Several hundred fighters and bombers were withdrawn from Norway, where they were not really needed, and brought south. Soon they were changing the balance of the war in the Mediterranean, attacking British shipping, bases and troop formations. In January 1941 the Flying Corps was moved to North Africa, and it was joined there by a panzer division commanded by Lieutenant-General Erwin Rommel.

From the north, through Bulgaria, the Germans began an attack on Greece and on Yugoslavia. The Luftwaffe had key roles in both. A thousand planes were employed to blast Belgrade, and then the panzers came rushing in. It was almost a duplication of the Polish campaign, and against the same sort of unprepared enemy. The result, in a propaganda sense, was to reinforce the image of Nazi invulnerability. Then came the campaign in Albania, in mainland Greece and in Crete, with the Luftwaffe dropping paratroops to take Crete. From Greece and the Dodecanese Islands, Stukas bombed. Ju-52s towed the gliders over Crete and let them go, and down they came onto the tiny, rough airfields. But the attackers had failed to reckon with the British defenses, and their losses were very heavy: a quarter of the paratroop force and 146 transport planes lost and 150 damaged. Hitler, always swift to jump to conclusions, decided that paratroops were of no use and refused to employ them further during the war, except as infantry.

In December 1940 Flight Cadet Heinz Knöke was finally assigned to the reserve squadron of No. 52 Fighter Wing at Krefeld. At last he was going to war. Like most of the operational fliers in Germany, Knöke recognized that the battle for Britain had ended—in a British victory. What would happen now, he could not conceive. But he would be in it, he knew.

In April 1941, Knöke was flying patrols over the southern coast of England. That became the routine; low-level missions over southern England, firing at flak emplacements and airfields, being attacked by Spitfires and fighting back. Then, suddenly, in June, Knöke's squadron had a strange order. They were assigned to shoot down the Douglas airliner on the Berlin-Moscow run. The commanding officer led a flight out, but they failed to find the Douglas. Still, when they came back, that was the talk of the mess. Something big must be about to happen.

17

SOVIET ADVENTURE

Adolf Hitler's paranoia about Communism paralleled his feelings for the Jews and made him unstable. His generals, and particularly Hermann Goering, knew that to attack the Soviet Union was madness, particularly when Germany was already waging an exhausting war on two fronts: in the Atlantic, against the Royal Navy and the RAF, and in the Mediterranean, where German army, Luftwaffe and U-boats were all deeply involved.

"We will smash the Russians before winter," Hitler predicted.

"But why attack?"

"Because if we don't attack them, they will attack us," Hitler said grimly, and he enumerated his reasons: the Soviets had permitted German engineers to inspect their armament factories—that meant they had something to hide; and besides that, the inspections had proved the Soviets were growing very strong. (What Hitler did not appreciate was that Stalin was showing him the Soviets' strength to deter him from attack.)

So the decision was made, and in spite of Goering's reminding Hitler of the fate of Napoleon, the Führer was relentless.

"Napoleon did not have the greatest army and the greatest air force in the world," said Hitler. "I have."

Goering was quick to agree with that last statement, and his good humor was restored. He seemed able to convince himself that in the end it would really work out all right.

The next step that spring was to convince the world that the Germans intended to move in the Mediterranean and against Britain. Goering made a speech in which he suggested that the invasion of Britain was not far off. But in fact everything had now been subordinated to Hitler's new plan, Operation Barbarossa, the assault on the Soviet Union. The Luftwaffe and Wehrmacht would combine forces as they had in Poland and in France, and they would smash the Soviets and move into the Caucasus. Hitler was talking about going as far as India.

Goering listened. But the fact was that he knew in his heart that the move east was a dreadful, fatal error, and he told General Kammhuber, one of his staff in the west, that he really washed his hands of the whole war effort at this point. That was not true—it could not be true: Hitler would never let Goering disassociate himself from the war, but the Reich Marshal knew better than Hitler the true state of the German economy and the ability to produce weapons, and that ability to do what Hitler wanted simply did not exist.

So Germany began living on promises, stealing from the west to feed the east, which worked for a while because Rommel was fighting gamely against great odds in the Mediterranean and doing wonders with very few resources. But this could last only so long. And also, the quiet that existed in western Europe could last only so long. While it lasted, Hitler could fool himself that the resources existed, and dream of taking the Caucasus oil and the Soviet steel and all the rest. But they were dreams, no more, and soon enough they would begin to turn to nightmares.

On June 1, Goering began moving many of his Luftwaffe squadrons east.

Lieutenant Knöke's 52nd Fighter Wing was transferred from Ostend to Suwalki, a former Polish air force base near the Soviet border, which it shared with Stukas and bombers. All sorts of rumors flowed through the camp, the most preposterous being the report that the Soviets were going to permit the Germans to cross the Caucasus to occupy the Dardanelles and the Middle East oil fields and seize the Suez Canal.

On June 22, having failed to shoot down the Berlin-Moscow airliner, the 52nd Wing was alerted at 4:00 A.M. At 4:30, the pilots assembled in the operations room for briefing. Then they learned that this was the day on which they were going to attack the Soviet Union.

At 5:00 A.M. Knöke's squadron took off, the fighters now equipped with bomb racks and each carrying 100 five-pound fragmentation bombs. Their mission would be to support the Wehrmacht as airborne artillery.

That morning the German panzer divisions led the Wehrmacht in three columns toward Leningrad, Moscow and the Ukraine.

Accompanied by Stukas, Knöke's squadron attacked a Soviet headquarters west of Druskieniki.

> *On Russian territory everything appears to be asleep. We locate the headquarters and fly low over the wooden buildings, but there is not a Russian soldier in sight. Swooping at one of the huts,*

*I press the bomb-release button, on the control
stick. I distinctly feel the aircraft lift as it gets rid
of the load. . . .*

*One of the huts is fiercely blazing. Vehicles
have been stripped of their camouflage and overturned by the blast. The Ivans have at last come to
life. The scene below is like an overturned ant-
heap, as they scurry about in confusion. Stepsons
of Stalin in their underwear flee for cover in the
woods. Light flak guns appear. I set my sights on
one of them and open up with machine guns and
both cannon. An Ivan at the gun falls to the
ground, still in underwear. . . .*

Knöke's squadron carried out more attacks, was back at
the base at 5:56, and at 6:30 that morning was in the air
again, back to that headquarters, to work it over again and
hit the woods in which the Russian vehicles had been hidden.
At 7:20, they returned to base. The efficient ground crews
serviced and rearmed the aircraft, and they were off again at
7:42, to hit that same headquarters. This time, when they left,
there was not a single building standing.

By the time the squadron returned to the Polish airfield,
new orders had come from the front. After a meal, the pilots
took off again at 10:07, heading for the Grodno-Zytomia-
Skidel-Szczucyn highway, which they found clogged with
Soviet vehicles. They bombed and strafed columns of horse-
drawn artillery on the road, creating enormous confusion.
They returned to base, and finally, at 8:00 P.M., launched
their last raid of the day. They had flown six missions in
sixteen hours, and they had seen nothing of the Soviet air
force.

Altogether that day Goering's boys had raided sixty airfields and several aircraft factories, and reported having destroyed 1,800 planes, most of them on the ground. The surprise in every aspect of the war was almost complete.

On the second day, 800 Soviet planes were destroyed, and in the next three days another 1,200 planes were destroyed. It was taking the Soviets a little while to get organized.

Knöke's squadron encountered their first Soviet planes on June 23, near Grodno. The planes they met were old and slow Rata Fighters. They were no match for the Messerschmitts.

RUSSIAN ROUT

One of the Russian planes had been hit, and was spiraling upward, trying to gain height, leaving a thick plume of black smoke behind it. Suddenly it lurched into an irrevocable dive towards the water. We saw a smaller shape detach from the mass of the plane—probably the pilot, trying to jump to safety. But his parachute, if he had one, failed to open. Man and machine hit the water at the same speed, and disintegrated.

—Guy Sajer, *The Forgotten Soldier*

So easy was the going that in a few weeks Luftwaffe units were being moved back to the west, where they were needed for escort duty and to combat the growing attacks by the British from the air. Lieutenant Knöke was transferred to the island of Borkum in the North Sea.

But now the Luftwaffe had an enormous problem. The number of planes available in the summer of 1941 was only a hundred greater than a year before, and now the German air war was being fought on three fronts—northwest Europe, the Mediterranean and the Soviet Union. The Luftwaffe actually had two hundred fewer bombers than it had in 1939 when the Polish campaign began.

The Luftwaffe sent three air fleets to support the Wehrmacht forces on the ground. Sixty-five percent of the Luftwaffe's strength was now committed against the Soviets. And facing them, although they did not know it, were eight thousand Soviet planes, against their force of less than three thousand aircraft.

But so slow were the Soviets to recover (Stalin had just recently purged his officer corps and murdered most of the best) that the Germans scored one victory after another, on the ground and in the air. At the end of the first week of operations, the Germans had wiped out about half the Soviet air strength.

OUTGUNNED IN THE AIR

Until the final stages of the war, Russian aircraft were no match for the *Luftwaffe*. Even in Prussia, where Russian airpower was its most active, the appearance of one Messerschmitt-109 or one Focke-Wulf would make a dozen armoured Ilyushin bombers turn and run.

—Guy Sajer, *The Forgotten Soldier*

On the ground, the panzers had advanced nearly 200 miles to the Dvina River and were moving into the Baltic. In less than three weeks the envelopment of Minsk cost the Soviets nearly 300,000 prisoners and 2,500 tanks. The Germans hurried on to Smolensk and took another 100,000 prisoners.

BLACK CROSSES RULE THE SKIES

Two of the remaining Yaks had taken flight, pursued by our planes, when the last dived straight at the convoy. One of the Focke-Wulfs was chasing him, and was plainly trying to get him in his sights.—The Soviet plane had come down very low, to use its machine guns. The trucks ahead of us had stopped short, and the able-bodied were jumping down into the mud.

—With my nose in the mud, my hands on my head, and my eyes instinctively shut, I heard the machine guns and the two planes through a hellish intensity of noise. The sound of racing engines was followed by a loud explosion. I looked up, to watch the plane with the black crosses on its wings regain altitude. Three or four hundred yards away, where the Yak had crashed, there was a plume of black smoke.

—Guy Sajer, *The Forgotten Soldier*

But as the German armies moved deeper into the Soviet Union, the task of the Luftwaffe grew greater.

As the German armies marched, behind them came the scavengers, organized by Goering to take over and exploit the resources of the captured territories. The political commissar was Erich Koch, an ardent Nazi who heeded some careless words dropped by Goering to "kill all the men in the Ukraine" as if they were gospel. He had two venal assistants, Fritz Sauckel, who was in charge of manpower, and Heinrich Himmler, who was at work solving "the Jewish problem" by killing as many Jews as possible. Goering, having put the wheels in motion by establishing the policy of utilizing the resources of the Ukraine, then paid little attention to the details.

Goering has been faulted for not paying attention, either, to the welfare of the Luftwaffe at this point. But that is a hasty criticism and does not take into account his extremely difficult position vis-à-vis Hitler, who, when he formulated the attack on the Soviet Union, seemed to have lost the last vestiges of his sanity. Goering had opposed the Soviet adventure from the beginning, based on his dislike of fighting a war on two fronts, but Hitler, backed by von Ribbentrop and Goebbels and a whole host of toadies, had opted for the attack as if it were a holy mission—which to Hitler it seemed to be—so great were his fear and detestation of Communism. What would come of all this, Goering did not know, other than Hitler's insistence that the Soviets must be "crushed."

The problem of the Luftwaffe in the spring of 1941 was lack of time and lack of preparation. Since 1936 they had been building furiously, planning and conducting research and development, despite Hitler's strictures against any development that would not put weapons immediately into the field. But it had been start and stop, and consequently the Germans were fighting in 1941 with the weapons of 1939, whereas their British enemies had improved their own weapons remarkably, and soon the USA would be supplying weapons that were even more modern.

A further difficulty was Hitler's growing tendency to consider himself the only general in the field. As of the summer of 1941, this had already cut the ground out from under the Luftwaffe. Hitler's insistence on the terror campaign against British cities had made it impossible for Goering to win the Battle of Britain. He never knew what Hitler would demand next. The Führer had already demanded the movement into the Mediterranean. What strategy would Hitler order next? And how and when? He changed his mind almost daily, and Goering could not gainsay him. So there was no point in Goering's holding conferences on strategy and tactics with his subordinates, because whatever they might decide was subject to the whim of Hitler. And the whimsicality increased month by month.

Just before the opening of the Soviet campaign, Hitler had called all his senior commanders together and told them that it was their sacred duty to destroy Communism. Later Field Marshal Keitel would say that this day was the beginning of the end, for from that time on Hitler's behavior became ever more irrational. Thus, when R. J. Overy, biographer of Goering, faults the Reich Marshal for failing to delegate authority and hold strategy meetings after 1941, this is unkind: if strategy meetings had been held, they would only have caused more frustration among the generals. From 1941, it was Hitler's war, and no one else's opinions mattered.

In the first three months of the war against the Soviets, the Luftwaffe won victories. But after that, the tide turned. The Russian autumn was marked by rains that turned the land into seas of mud and immobilized the panzer divisions. Then overnight the mud froze, and the snows came down and the Russian winter began. The Germans had not planned to be standing still in mid-Russia in the winter, and they were not dressed for the weather, nor were their vehicles prepared. Back in Berlin, Dr. Goebbels organized a campaign to persuade the public to donate furs and warm clothing to the soldiers at the front, and soon the men were wearing civilian coats, furs and mittens.

Soon the Luftwaffe began to suffer shortages. Part of the reason was Goering's bad management of the general economy. Or was it bad? The fact is that the German economy was strained to the breaking point and had been since the war began. The generals of the Wehrmacht and Goering had not wanted or expected war until the mid-1940s, by which time they could have built reserves of everything necessary. But Hitler, who had staged those magnificent bluffs in 1935 and 1938, knowing that if the Allies stood up to him he would have to back down because of the weakness of his military machine, was persuaded by Goebbels and von Ribbentrop to continue his adventures in 1939. There was no time to build reserves, and by 1941 it was all the air factories could do to keep supplying enough planes to retain the levels of the years before. There were not enough aircraft engines to replace worn-out or damaged ones; consequently by 1942 perhaps thirty percent of the aircraft were not operational, waiting for engines.

And the organization of the Luftwaffe suffered sorely from bad management. Goering liked fighting men and did not have a great deal of patience with ground corps. Key staff jobs were given to fliers who often did not have the administrative abilities to handle them. Ernst Udet, the World War I pilot who had been appointed technical chief of the Luftwaffe in 1936, mismanaged that post for five years and finally, in 1941, committed suicide. Consequently the production schedules were a shambles, so much so that the new Me jet fighter, on which the Luftwaffe was counting, never went into serious production.

By the middle of 1941 even Hitler and Goering sensed that something was dreadfully wrong with production, and Goering turned the management over to Milch. The result was salutary: at the Siebel works the mechanization of wing assemblies for the Ju-88 meant a 250 percent increase in output with no more labor or expense.

By the autumn of 1941 supply had become the biggest problem of the Luftwaffe in the east. Between August 10 and 21 the 8th Flying Corps, which was assigned to cut the Moscow-Leningrad railway line, lost ten percent of its aircraft and saw fifty-four percent damaged.

During that period the army bogged down at Smolensk. It got going again at the end of August and drove to the suburbs of Leningrad. There the army stopped at Hitler's order and was told not to capture the city. Hitler wanted to make a terrible example of Leningrad, to frighten the Soviet people into submission. He insisted that the army stop, and create a siege and starve out the people in Leningrad.

In the south, General Guderian's Panzer Group 2 broke loose and moved south to join up with General von Kleist's Panzer Group 1, thus encircling hundreds of thousands of Soviets. They took 655,000 prisoners. That autumn Guderian's group moved back north, captured Orel and Bryansk and disrupted the Russian center. A column was marching on Moscow and in November Hitler announced to the world that the Soviets were finished.

The air war was lost in 1941, when the Germans failed to keep up with the technological developments of their enemies. The aircraft the Luftwaffe destroyed so easily in the early days of the Soviet fighting were mostly obsolete, and a whole new generation of fast, sleek Soviet planes were in the works. The Germans failed to produce a heavy bomber at all. The He-177 was a failure, because Ernst Udet had been wedded to the dive-bombing technique and insisted that this bomber dive. The Ju-288 also failed, and the Me-210 was discarded in 1942 because it had so many problems. Thus the Germans were in the poor position of continuing to fight the war with less-than-modern weapons.

This fact was not yet apparent. The Wehrmacht seemed to

be driving to victory that late autumn of 1941, but already the Allies were outproducing Germany: in the coming year they would produce 100,000 aircraft, while Germany and her allies would produce 26,000.

By the last day of October the German drive had slackened. The weather turned foul, and the Luftwaffe planes were now flying from dirt strips that turned to mud, and individual flights dropped from 1,000 to 250 a day.

In the autumn of 1941 Goering's relations with Hitler worsened steadily. One reason was the appointment of Martin Bormann as Hitler's deputy, after Rudolf Hess took it into his head to fly to Britain on a personal peace mission and was captured and held in the Tower of London instead. Hitler appointed Bormann over Goering's objections, and Bormann never forgot that. From that point on, he had the knife out for "the Iron Man," as Hitler called Goering, and it was not long before Hitler was referring to the Reich Marshal as *"der Dicke"* ("Fatty").

Hitler's sharp tongue so often irritated Goering that in this autumn of 1941 Goering more or less stopped attending the Führer's daily situation conferences at the Chancellery, and sent General Bodenschatz, his old friend from World War I, to represent him most of the time.

The Goering-Hitler relationship hit a new low one day, when Hitler had one of his brainstorms. He was bent on starving the Soviet people, to get rid of them and provide more food for the Germans after the Soviets were defeated. But wouldn't it be even better to knock them out with a big blow? Hitler chose a day when Goering was at the conference and proposed that blow: Goering was to withdraw all aircraft from western Europe and Africa and concentrate them in the east. He was to strike a massive blow in a series of air raids against Moscow and Leningrad. Both cities were to be totally destroyed, the buildings razed to the ground and the populations wiped out.

When Hitler made this suggestion at the conference, Bormann was loud in praise of the "brilliant" idea. The others at the meeting were noncommittal, and they turned to Goering, awaiting his reaction.

Goering told Hitler that it would be the height of folly to withdraw aircraft from all the other fronts. Hitler persisted. Finally Goering said it would be impossible. Hitler was furious, accusing Goering and the Luftwaffe of cowardice. Hitler then turned away and would not speak to Goering or look at him again during that meeting.

Then Goering got into very deep trouble with Hitler. The administrators of the Ukraine were now in situ: Koch—hard, wizen-faced—and Heinrich Himmler. They were killing off or shipping to slave-labor camps the able-bodied men of the Ukraine when Alfred Krupp, who had been placed by Goering in charge of turning Soviet production there to German use, objected that they were stealing his labor. Goering interceded and stopped the murder and the shipment of men to Germany. Hitler did not like it, but Goering had his way because he held that the move was necessary for the good of the Third Reich.

But Goering's worst sin in Hitler's eyes was yet to come. As the Russian winter began and the aircraft engines seized up or would not start in the cold, Goering went to Hitler to ask him to stop pressing the war farther into the Soviet Union.

The Luftwaffe General Staff, just then, was beginning to realize that it needed a respite from the enormous drain on its resources, time in which it could build planes for the future and not just keep one jump ahead of the casualty rate.

Goering suggested building an East Wall, like the Siegfried Line, along the border of the territory captured by November. The Luftwaffe would protect that line, but the Luftwaffe could not continue to move inland into the Soviet Union. It did not have the resources for further expansion at this point.

Hitler was furious with Goering for asking him to stop. What Goering did not know was that Hitler was hearing the same arguments from the generals of Wehrmacht, whose tanks and trucks were freezing up and whose men were dropping from frostbite. General von Kleist's panzers were on a line at the Mius River and wanted to remain there. Field Marshal von Rundstedt wanted to make this the winter line, but even this could not be held. The Soviets had regained strength, were building tanks and aircraft furiously and launched their winter offensive. Von Rundstedt said he was going to retreat further.

Hitler became furious and ordered von Rundstedt to hold at all costs. "Remain where you are and retreat no further. . . ."

Von Rundstedt said no; if Hitler did not rescind the order, he was quitting his command.

"Fine," said Hitler. "Please give up your command."

He then told Field Marshal von Kluge to begin a winter offensive. It started in November, just as the winter arrived, with −30°C weather and a major Soviet attack. The Germans fell back in disarray. Their casualties were now a million men since the beginning of the Soviet adventure, a million men in six months, and still Hitler would not listen to reason.

It was just then that Goering had made his stand, and he reaped the reward of Hitler's anger. Never again would his relationship with Hitler be close.

18

THE FRONTS CRUMBLE

On 7 December 1941, Japanese carrier bombers opened the war against the Western powers with an attack on Pearl Harbor in Hawaii, and almost simultaneously attacked the Philippines, Malaya and the Dutch East Indies. Within a few hours two major British warships, the *Repulse* and the *Prince of Wales,* were sunk by Japanese land-based aircraft. All of this was good news for the Germans, because it meant Britain would now be fighting on two fronts. But what many in Germany could not understand was why Hitler decided to declare war on the United States.

HITLER STRIKES FIRST

I suppose that the Führer declared war on America because he believed that Roosevelt would declare war on Germany if he didn't, and Hitler wanted to get his blow in first.

—Goering

It was true that the Germans were bound to Japan by the Tripartite Pact with Italy. But it was also true that, when Hitler had invaded the Soviet Union, the Japanese had felt no compulsion to go to war with Stalin. So the obligation was not real. The reason for Hitler's declaration had to be from a sense of exasperation, and the proddings of Admiral Dönitz, whose U-boats had actually been at war with the Americans for almost a year. But it was a most shortsighted policy declaration, because it meant that almost immediately the Soviets would be receiving war materials from the U.S., as the British had for two years.

Hitler had expected the Americans to devote their major war effort to the Japanese front, but he failed to recognize the persuasive powers of Winston Churchill, who, within a few days, had talked American President Franklin D. Roosevelt around to exerting America's major effort in Europe and only holding in the Far East until that situation could be dealt with later. Given the global nature of the new war, it was a sensible decision, if costly to the Americans in the Philippines and to the Dutch and British in Asia. The tide of Japanese expansion was immediate but limited. Hitler's expansion threatened the entire world.

By the beginning of 1942, the situation in the Soviet Union had changed completely. The Germans had nearly reached Moscow and Leningrad, and they had penetrated deep into the southern underbelly of the Soviet Union. But at Stalingrad, Moscow and Leningrad the Soviets vowed to hold (Stalin said he would not leave Moscow), and they did hold. From factories in the east, aircraft and tanks began to push toward the German front. These were modern machines, bigger and more powerful than anything the Germans had. Hitler expressed surprise when his generals told him the

Soviets had better equipment and more of it than he. They had been trying to tell him something about the Soviet potential for months, but he had steadfastly refused to listen, and now it was the same.

German aircraft production and training now fell behind the losses. The first sign came in January 1942, when it was announced that the training program for pilots would be shortened by a month—in order to get air crews into the eastern sector. By March 1942 it was impossible for the Luftwaffe to forecast how many crew and planes would be available in the next three months.

Now came a new failure. Goering had presided over the policy adopted toward the new colonies of the Third Reich. France, for example, had a big aircraft industry, which might have been turned to the use of the Third Reich, as had the Czechoslovak industry. But instead of maintaining the French industry, Goering allowed its cannibalization, with raw materials and machine tools and other resources torn from their French roots and shipped to Germany, along with the forced labor needed to work the tools. It did not work out. The aircraft industries of the occupied countries produced virtually nothing for the Germans. The Netherlands, with their Fokker plants, produced only sixteen planes in 1941. France produced sixty-two.

Hitler's mania about the Soviets also militated against the successful employment of prisoners of war as labor. By the end of 1941, the Germans claimed to have captured four million prisoners in the Soviet Union. But of these, two-thirds had already starved to death as a result of Hitler's no-food policy, and only 400,000 were even capable of moving. Hitler did not want them in Germany, but the German industrialists did, and they told him that unless he gave them labor they could not give him the munitions he wanted, so reluctantly he acceded to the demands for Soviet labor. But it was really too late. Goering had to accept a large share of the blame for this situation, because he knew the industrial problems and yet he did not stand up to Hitler to prevent the murder of millions of prisoners.

THE POWER OF STARVATION

Goering told me that hunger among the Russian prisoners had reached such an extreme that in order to start them toward the interior it is no longer necessary to send them under armed guard; it is enough to put at the head of the column of prisoners a camp kitchen, which emits the fragrant odor of food; thousands and thousands of prisoners trail along like a herd of famished animals.

—Galiazzo Ciano, Italian Foreign Minister

After Udet's suicide, Field Marshal Milch readjusted the Luftwaffe's production priorities, and the situation began to improve. They called the plan the Goering Plan, and it demanded thirty percent more production in 1942.

As 1942 began, so did the German debacle. The Soviets launched a major counteroffensive, and the Germans could not stand up against it, but Hitler demanded that his generals refuse to retreat. The argument grew bitter. General von Brauchitsch was dismissed, and Hitler assumed complete control of the Wehrmacht high command for himself.

The panzer divisions almost ceased to exist. Their tanks froze, and their riflemen dropped from frostbite. At the end of the year the 6th Panzer Division had no tanks, and the 7th Panzer Division had a combat strength of 200 men.

That winter six German divisions, 100,000 men, were surrounded in the Demyansk area. To Goering's Luftwaffe came the task of supplying them if they were to survive. A similar situation existed in the Kholm area. The Luftwaffe did not have any real system of airlift, but one was improvised, and this enabled the ground troops to hold out until May, when relieving forces could break through to them. The airlift flew 14,000 missions and moved 24,000 tons of supply to Demyansk; 15,000 reinforcements were moved in and 23,000 casualties taken out. The missions averaged more than a hundred per day and moved 265 tons per day. But the cost was very high: thirty percent of the Luftwaffe's transport force was lost by February. And to keep the planes flying, the training schools were decimated.

So it could be seen that the survival of the German armies under the conditions was a matter of error: the error of Stalin in overruling Marshal Zhukov and doing just what Hitler had done—biting off more than he could chew. Thus, while the Soviet offensive of the winter of 1942 pushed the Germans back everywhere, there was not enough Soviet strength exerted at any one point to make a complete breakthrough, and so, in spite of himself, Hitler survived.

But he had learned nothing: so much was soon apparent. Field Marshal Halder, who remained as Chief of Staff, suggested that it would be wise to spend the next year rebuilding along the eastern wall; the Germans would refrain from any offensives but would build strength. Hitler scoffed. His generals knew nothing. He was poised to make a knockout blow against Stalin. All he needed was a few skillful commanders.

On 5 April 1942, Hitler issued Directive No. 41, calling for a summer offensive, although of the 162 divisions in the east only eight were in shape for offensive operations. Hitler would use Italians and Romanians to build up his manpower. The German generals had no confidence at all in these allies, but Hitler would not listen to reason.

The forces in the north would move to link up the Leningrad front with Finland. The center forces, smashed in the winter's fighting, would not move. In the south, Hitler would try to penetrate the Caucasus and secure control of its precious oil.

The task for Goering's Luftwaffe was to support this southern advance. The planes were to fly close support of the troops, and also to blast Soviet railway traffic. The Luftwaffe was expected to maintain control of the air.

Before the summer offensive in the east could begin, Hitler and Goering received a big shock in the west. For two years the British had been fighting back, with air raids on various German cities, mostly at night, but these had been regarded as mostly nuisances. But on the night of May 30 RAF bombers raided Cologne in the Ruhr basin and dropped 1,500 tons of bombs.

The next day Goering, as usual, did not attend the Führer situation conference but sent General Bodenschatz and General Jeschonnek. The latter had to read the report of the bombing: "We estimate that 200 enemy aircraft . . ." He did not get much further. Hitler already had a report from his *Gauleiter* in the area. "There were a thousand or more English aircraft," the *Gauleiter* had reported. The damage was terrible. Could not something be done?

Bodenschatz slipped out of the room and called Goering at his headquarters. Goering hurried to the meeting but when he got there Hitler would not speak to him.

Goering did his best that summer. He tried to be everywhere and do everything, but the situation grew steadily

---

A FATAL DENIAL

Back in 1940 Goering had boasted that never a bomb would drop on Germany. Now it appeared that over 1,000 planes had dropped a huge tonnage on Cologne; he wouldn't have it. His reputation was at stake. "The report from your police commissioner is a stinking lie!" he bellowed over the phone. "I tell you as Reichsmarschall that the figures cited are simply too high. How can you dare to report such fantasies to the Führer?"

Shouting and screaming into the phone, he ordered Grohé to change his figures.

—Charles Whiting, *The Three Star Blitz*

---

worse. It was certainly noticeable to Hitler, because the Americans came in with the big B-17 bombers and their daylight raids. By autumn the trouble was growing worse. One day, when Goering was at Carinhall, the bombers raided. He went down into the shelter underneath, with Emmy and several others. One of the crowd started to talk about what she was going to do when the Germans had won the war.

"Can't you realize that we have already lost the war?" Goering said. "It is already lost, but the Führer refuses to recognize the fact."

And of course it was true. The Luftwaffe had never been designed to be a complete force, only a striking air force, to support the Wehrmacht in lightning attack. Without heavy bombers, with fighters that grew less imposing every time the Allies brought forth a new one, the German air force was in trouble all the time. But worse now was the inability to catch up, no matter how much effort was put into aircraft production, because of the unceasing new demands of the Führer for impossibilities.

That summer on the southern front the German armies moved against the Soviets again, and they won a victory. They captured 200,000 Soviet prisoners. Von Richthofen's Stuka went after the city of Sevastopol and virtually leveled it in five days of air bombardment accompanied by artillery firing, beginning on June 2.

So by summer 1942, the Luftwaffe, which was supposed to put 3,000 planes into the air, was able to muster only 1,500 in support of the offensive. As the Germans surged forward, this time the Soviets gave ground and escaped the traps. The Luftwaffe did a fine job of supporting the ground troops, and the Germans inflicted serious losses on the Soviets, but the result was constant attrition of the German air force once again. From May to September 1942, the Luftwaffe bomber groups lost 120 bombers per month, and the fighters lost the same number. By autumn the commanders were describing the state of the Luftwaffe in the east as "strained."

As the Germans advanced on the Caucasus, Hitler became enamored of the city of Stalingrad. In the third week of August, with a large force in control north of the city, the German attack began. Von Richthofen's 4th Air Fleet started a major attack on Stalingrad, bombing and strafing, and from this point Stalingrad dominated German activity on the Soviet front. By the end of October 1942 the Germans had captured most of the city, but the Soviets held on to the banks of the Volga River. And the Germans were at the end of a very long supply line. Beginning in November, the Soviets threw much more air support into the battle, and their aircraft challenged the Luftwaffe's control of the skies. Soviet planes were cutting up the supply caravans to the front. What had appeared to be an easy victory suddenly became a serious struggle.

Over Europe, the sky was full of Allied bombers. The British, using the plywood Mosquito light bomber, were particularly annoying in their harrying of Berlin.

One day in November, Lieutenant Knöke was serving as temporary flight commander of a special unit of the 12th Air Corps in the Netherlands. As night fell, he had a telephone call from Colonel Henschel, commander of the fighter defenses.

"How is the weather?" asked the colonel.

"Just as bad as it can be, sir. I can only see a few yards."

"You will have to fly, and that is all there is to it. I have just had a call from Reich Marshal Goering. He is in one of his rages. Why are we not in the air? The weather is too bad for us to fly; yet those confounded Tommies can get over Berlin. Do you imagine I would tell that to the Reich Marshal? Those Mosquitoes are to be shot down at all costs. Do you understand?"

"Yes, sir."

And that night Knöke's unit flew. He shot down one Mosquito himself.

In the autumn of 1942, the German situation in Africa changed for the worse. General Rommel was doing wonders with his small force, but he needed help. Field Marshal Kesselring tried to give it to him, but there were not enough aircraft available, and they faced two of Britain's smartest air commanders, General Arthur Tedder and General Coningham. The RAF in the Mediterranean was stronger than the Luftwaffe in terms both of numbers and of quality. The British were sinking a third of the ships sent from Italy to Libya, then they were sinking two-thirds, and finally at the end of 1941 they were sinking three-quarters of the tonnage dispatched.

Kesselring sent the 2nd Air Fleet to the African area in November of 1941, the pressure was removed, the ships began to get through and in the spring of 1942 the Luftwaffe and the Italians began the siege of Malta. By May the siege was so successful that Malta was virtually on the verge of starvation. But Hitler then vetoed an invasion. He no longer trusted the airborne troops—for no good reason, since they had performed admirably at Crete. Because the Führer opted against invasion, the Luftwaffe had to maintain strong forces in Sicily to keep up the pressure on Malta.

By midsummer, Hitler's draining of the Reich's resources to support his eastern dream had brought disaster upon disaster. Rommel reported that he could no longer hold against the growing strength of the British without help from air and sea. The help was not forthcoming, and the El Alamein front collapsed. Shipping began to build up in the Mediterranean, and someone suggested that the Allies might be planning a landing in Algeria and Morocco.

Nonsense! said Hitler. Goering concurred. The West was not powerful enough. But a week later the landing came.

The French soon gave in and joined the Allies. The Germans occupied Tunisia and dealt the Americans a shrewd blow at Kasserine Pass, but Rommel could not exploit the victory, because he had to rush back to meet a new challenge from General Bernard Montgomery's British Eighth Army. Everywhere it was the same: the German forces had too little with which to operate; they were strung too thin across the lines. In Africa they depended on the Italians. In the Soviet Union the great Sixth Army was bogged down in Stalingrad, and Hitler would not let it escape from that trap. To the south lay the Romanian Fourth Army, which Goering did not trust. To the north, up against the Don River, lay the Hungarian Second, the Italian Eighth and Romanian Third Armies, not one of which the German field marshals expected to fight in a crisis.

As anticipated, on 19 November 1942 four Soviet armies smashed the Romanian Third Army. In less than a day the Romanians collapsed, and the Soviets started to drive swiftly southeast and rolled up the 22nd Panzer Division. That first afternoon Hitler learned that affairs were not going well. By the next day two Soviet armies jolted the Romanians south of Stalingrad, and that Romanian army promptly collapsed. Now the Sixth Army was threatened by a pincer movement. The hope was to get out quickly from Stalingrad. Hitler flatly refused to let the Sixth Army escape when it could. "I will not leave the Volga," he said. On November 23 the Sixth Army was surrounded. Hitler told them to stand fast. He called Goering to come from Luftwaffe headquarters to the Oberkommando Wehrmacht (OKW, Supreme Command) command post.

In the meantime, General von Richthofen, whose 4th Air Fleet was supporting von Paulus' Sixth Army, warned von Paulus that the Luftwaffe did not have the resources to resupply the army during the winter and that von Paulus must break out of the trap to save himself. But von Paulus' chief of staff said there was no other way than by aerial resupply.

When Goering reached OKW headquarters, Hitler asked him if he could do the job.

Goering's answer was an unequivocal "Yes."

GOERING'S PROMISE

My leader! I personally guarantee the supplying of Stalingrad by air. You can rely on that.

—Goering to Hitler

The trouble with that answer was that it did not coincide with the facts. Goering by this time did not even know the capabilities of his air force on the eastern front, so bemused was he with economic problems in Germany. He was counting on his intuition and a miracle. The Luftwaffe had succeeded in Demyansk and Kholm the previous winter, and now General Jeschonnek agreed with Goering that it could be done.

However, not only did the tides of war go against the Germans, causing withdrawal of reserves and units scheduled for the eastern front in order to shore up the German operations in Africa and Sicily, where the Allies now attacked, but the winter went against them, too. This winter was unusually severe, even for Russia. The Soviets made a deep encirclement around Stalingrad, seizing the airfields the 4th Air Fleet had planned to use for winter operations. Von Richthofen had to put together new airfields.

On 23 November 1942, Goering ordered the air-transports force to begin supplying the Sixth Army in Stalingrad. The army said it needed 600 tons of supply a day. Scores of planes capable of carrying supplies were diverted from bombing and other tasks and shifted to the east. But first, before they could help, they had to fly more than 1,250 miles to reach the front line. Many planes and crews were lost in shipment. And when they arrived, they found flying conditions so appalling that operational rates were seldom more than fifty percent. Not until December did the number of transports reach 200. Instead of 600 tons of supply a day, they were delivering only 350 tons on the best days, and sometimes none at all.

In spite of Hitler's insistence that nothing be done except that von Paulus must hold out, the German generals launched a relief expedition toward Stalingrad. It came close, to Mishkova, only thirty-five miles from the besieged area. Hitler's generals urged him to authorize a breakout. Hitler would not. Von Paulus would not move without Hitler's permission. So the army remained when it could have escaped.

One by one the airfields from which von Richthofen supplied the Sixth Army began to fall under Soviet onslaught. Von Richthofen appealed to Goering, who said he was worrying too much. The major field at Tatsinskaya fell, then the field at Morozovskaya, and the transport planes were operating from the field at Novocherkassk, 220 miles from Stalingrad. By mid-January 1943, the major airfield receiving supplies had fallen, and thereafter supply was by airdrop, much of which was lost.

On February 2, von Paulus surrendered after a series of powerful Soviet attacks. Hitler was furious, not with himself for ordering the foolish stand, not with Goering for promising what he could not deliver, but with von Paulus for choosing to save as many men as he could from death.

For the Luftwaffe, Stalingrad was as great a disaster as it was for the Wehrmacht. Into the bin of destruction went 269 Ju-52s, 169 He-111s and 157 other types of planes. The loss was as great as if an entire Flying Corps had been thrown away.

After the loss of Stalingrad, the Germans in the north-central front rallied and launched a counteroffensive that was quite successful. They drove the Soviets back toward Kharkov and in March captured that city. The Luftwaffe averaged a thousand sorties per day in support of this army operation, and their efforts were successful, since the Soviets had run their armies beyond their air capability. But this was the last German offensive on Soviet soil. And for the Luftwaffe it was also very near the end. At noon on 27 January 1943, the war over northern Europe became a new nightmare for the men of the Luftwaffe.

Here is Lieutenant Knöke's recollection:

> At noon comes the first attack by American bombers on the North Sea Coast of Germany. We have been expecting it for several weeks. The enemy consists of formation of heavy four-engine Consolidated Liberators and Boeing B-17s. The Boeings are known, and with good reason, as "Flying Fortresses" and that is exactly what they are with exceptionally heavy defensive armament which creates some very severe problems for our Fighter control.
>
> Our intelligence service has kept us supplied for months with a constant flow of information about these giant planes. Bit by bit we are able to familiarize ourselves with every technical detail of their performance. As fighter pilots we are particularly interested in the defensive armament. Sixteen superheavy machine guns are so arranged that no blind spot is left anywhere within range of the aircraft. . . .
>
> It is obvious to me that today, with the first

massed daylight attack by the Americans, on Germany, marks the opening of a new phase of the war in the air. . . .

In 1943 the greatest land battle of the war began, in the Kursk-Orel area. The Germans fought very fiercely, but the Russians overpowered them, and soon Kharkov and Belgorod fell. In September, Army Group South began to unravel.

And so did the Luftwaffe in the east. At the end of June nearly forty percent of the total aircraft of the Luftwaffe were in the east, and that included eighty-five percent of the dive-bombers and thirty-three percent of the other bombers. Only twenty-seven percent of the fighters were in the east, because so many were needed to intercept the American and British bombers that were now working over Germany, and also to fight the war in the Sicilian and then Italian fronts.

Hitler had opted to expand his war in 1941, and he had put the Luftwaffe in the position of fighting on three major fronts: North Europe, Africa and South Europe, and the east. As the pressure grew in the east, so, too, did it grow in the west and south. Goering's Luftwaffe just could not handle all the tasks.

Because of the American landings and the big supply buildup in the Mediterranean, the Germans had to shut down their attacks on the Murmansk convoys to send units to the Mediterranean. The Luftwaffe began to feel the force of Hitler's decision to war with America, when American planes began arriving in large number in the Mediterranean and in Britain. By the summer of 1943 the strategic bombing campaign against German industry was getting into full swing, and in the summer of 1943, on the eve of the Sicilian invasion, the 2nd Air Fleet was divided into two parts, one to control Italy and the other the Balkans. This split did not help. Close to forty percent of all German fighter production had to be sent south, and much of it was lost in the campaign that followed.

The Allies quickly established air superiority in the Sicilian campaign. After that they soon controlled the air over Italy, so that the German Luftwaffe withdrew almost entirely by midsummer 1943, in spite of Hitler's orders that no units were to withdraw anywhere. The result of the Führer's stubbornness was that the squadrons lost most of their ground crews and most of their equipment. Hitler was moving from one disaster to another, and in these days his basic orders precluded Goering's being much more to the Luftwaffe than a highly decorated office boy.

Many changes had come to Goering in these months. In the spring of 1942, his title as head of the Four-Year Plan had become more or less meaningless, when Albert Speer was made minister of production under Hitler. Speer was a good politician, and he mollified Goering by setting up a central planning board and electing Goering chairman, sure that as soon as Goering had the title he would not interfere with operations. He was right. Goering never did interfere.

More acquaintances began to notice that Goering did not seem to have much interest in the conduct of the war anymore. He knew it was lost. He knew what had happened to his Luftwaffe and that it could never triumph over the combined air might of the east and west. He, who had collected titles and jobs the way a gambler collects betting cards, now began to divest himself of them.

In the spring of 1942 he had cast off the manpower assignment, which put control of the Jews and the enslaved populations into the hands of Fritz Sauckel. As soon as this happened, the Nazis in charge of murder stepped up the pace; Goering had been a restraining influence, if not from conscience. But there was a bit of conscience left, for when Goering heard that the Gestapo and the Himmler organization were shipping workers to the gas ovens, he protested in the name of production. For a while Himmler and Sauckel slowed down again, but then, in the autumn of 1942, they received an order direct from Hitler, and that superseded anything Goering might say, so the murders increased a hundredfold.

BLIND FAITH

I have no conscience, Adolf Hitler is my conscience.

—Goering

Everywhere in the autumn of 1942 and thereafter, Hitler was besieged, and so was Goering. In North Africa, he promised Field Marshal Rommel the moon and gave him a moonbeam. At a meeting between the Führer, Rommel and Goering, the latter was told to give Rommel what he wanted. And he said, "I will attend to it myself."

But what he did not say was that he had virtually nothing to give. Even his own personal unit, the Hermann Goering Panzer Division, was committed to the North African campaign and then the Sicilian campaign, and then the Italian campaign. . . .

He gave Field Marshal Rommel a ride in the famous Goering armored train from the Führer's headquarters at Rastenburg down to Rome, where he wanted to go on a shopping trip and where Rommel was going to emplane for North Africa and the final days of the lost campaign. Rommel wanted to talk about supply. All Goering would talk about was precious stones and fine paintings. Goering was not being stupid or evasive. The Reich was in trouble, and no one knew it better than the Reich Marshal. What could he say to Rommel? That he could see the end? For that was the real truth of 1942 in the Third Reich.

19

HOW THE LUFTWAFFE FAILED

On that day in 1918 when Captain Hermann Goering turned over the planes of his fighter squadron to the French, the German Flying Corps had ceased to exist, and the terms of the Versailles treaty were very strict and very specific: Germany was forbidden to have an air force.

But in the 1920s General Hans von Seeckt, the commander in chief of the small army Germany was permitted to retain, made sure that the concept of air power would not be lost. He kept 180 officers in the army who had experience in the old Flying Corps, so that tradition would not be lost forever. And secretly von Seeckt arranged for subsidies for the infant German airline Lufthansa and for German firms manufacturing various airplane parts. For, while the Germans were forbidden to manufacture airplanes as such, they were not forbidden to make components. All of which shows the futility of trying in a treaty to forbid the recuperation of a defeated nation. The Germans went to Switzerland, to the Netherlands and to the USSR, and continued to make planes.

Anthony Fokker, the Dutch designer who had made the German Flying Corps so famous, continued to build aircraft, and his Fokkers became famous in South American airlines. As for German airlines, by 1927 Lufthansa and the others were flying more air miles per year than the British, French and Italians put together.

So in 1933, when the Nazis became powerful, and Hermann Goering persuaded Hitler that Germany needed immediately to create an air force, the framework was there. Glider enthusiasts, supported also by subsidies from the army, had created a corps of young men who knew a great deal about aerodynamics, if they had not experienced flight in a motorized plane. From the army Goering drew a core of officers who soon learned about aircraft. By October 1933, 228 of the most talented army officers had been persuaded to transfer to the Luftwaffe.

So it was not quite correct to say, as the cynics did, that "Germany has an Imperial navy, a Prussian army and a Nazi air force." Also Goering brought into the new air force many friends from the old Flying Corps, including his old adjutant and such men as Ernst Udet, an artist among airmen, if no administrator. Udet served well, if only to bring to Germany the Stuka dive-bomber, but as an administrator and head of the technical department of the Luftwaffe he turned out to be a disaster, and when he realized it he killed himself.

A major problem of the German air force from the very beginning was the lack of a sense of mission. Goering knew what he wanted and needed: his experience in World War I showed that Germany needed a large number of strategic bombers, to carry out the long war (perhaps ten or twelve years) that Hitler envisaged for the 1940s. Hitler agreed with him completely. And yet, despite that decision at the top, Germany never did get a fleet of heavy bombers.

Why not?

For one reason, because Ernst Udet, who was in charge of

development, believed in dive-bombers, not in heavy-level bombers. In 1933 the heavy bomber program began well enough. A four-engine bomber, called the Uralbomber (even then Hitler was planning his war against the Soviet Union), was started on the road to construction. By 1936 the Junker and Dornier firms had two designs ready, the Ju-89 and the Do-19. Both prototypes were workable, although their engines were too small to do the job.

But Goering himself intervened. Instead of ordering work to build more powerful engines, he stopped the construction of the heavy bombers. The reason was his preoccupation with the Four-Year Plan and his need to allocate funds and personnel on a priority basis. He saw greater needs than that for a long-range bomber, and so everything was put in abeyance.

The real villain of this piece was Albert Kesselring. The first chief of staff of the Luftwaffe was Major-General Walther Wever, an extremely competent organizer who saw what Hitler and Goering wanted, and agreed with them. But he died on 3 May 1936 and was succeeded by Albert Kesselring, who did not share Wever's enthusiasm for the heavy bomber. He was inclined to favor Udet's belief in the dive-bomber as the instrument of the future. So it was really at his request that Goering first ordered the work stopped on the heavy bombers.

General Milch, who was Goering's personal representative, then completed the sabotage of the four-engine bomber. One of the major advocates of the bomber was Air Force General Deichmann. He was upset by Kesselring's actions, and he asked for a meeting with Goering on the subject, at which he expounded on the great value of the four-engine bomber, its performance and its worth. Then General Milch interrupted and said that the engineers of the air ministry did not think much of the four-engine bomber. Deichmann said that that was true but that the engineers of the technical office of the Luftwaffe were very high on the big bomber.

Perhaps, said Milch, but all available production money was needed to build up the fleet of Ju-88 medium twin-engine bombers.

In summary, General Milch pointed out the following facts:

1. The much-vaunted advantages of the four-engine bomber were overrated both in Germany and abroad.
2. What would be the point of being able to fly at 32,800 feet? According to statistics, the sky over Germany was overcast for so many days per year that it would be impossible to aim bombs from this altitude. (Milch exaggerated by forty percent.)
3. Germany's industrial capacity would permit a fleet of only a thousand four-engine bombers, while several times that many twin-engine bombers could be produced. The development of the heavy-bomber program, even on test models, would endanger the Ju-88 program.

It was this last argument that was effective with Goering. So Milch had persuaded Goering to change his mind.

It was not long, however, before the air force General Staff began to call for development of a long-range bomber. If they were to fight Britain and the Soviet Union, they would need just such a weapon. Goering, of course, believed that, but he did not want to spend the resources to build a four-engine bomber. The Heinkel people said they could build a long-range bomber with twice as much range as the four-engine one planned, and do it with two engines. Goering jumped at that idea. Heinkel then put forth a test model, the He-119. The machine would be called the He-177. Really it was a four-engine machine, with two sets of engines in a tandem arrangement. Thus it was neither fish nor fowl, rather a throwback to the World War I vintage of aircraft.

So the long-range bomber idea was resolved by pretending to work on a bomber but really not doing so. After 1938 Hitler's interest was minimal, because he was getting everything he wanted by bluffing and did not believe there would be a war with Britain.

When war with Britain did come, to everyone's surprise, work began again on the heavy bomber. But the dive-bombers proved so successful in Poland and France that once again the work was suspended, and when the bombing of Britain began, and the Ju-88 proved capable of flying to London and back, production of the heavy bomber was again postponed.

What the Germans had learned in Spain was the efficacy of the dive-bomber that Ernst Udet had so confidently advocated. So in the summer of 1939 the Luftwaffe developed the close-support idea, working with the panzer units. General von Richthofen, the latest of that illustrious line, was put in charge of this development. So successful was the Luftwaffe in disorganizing the Polish cavalry and infantry and hitting Polish airfields that, as noted, the world was astonished by the speed of Germany's blitzkrieg.

The same tactics were enormously successful in France, and later in Greece and Crete. A special unit was created in Poland, the Eighth Air Force. So successful was it in the blitzkrieg operation that no one could deny it. A few lowly heads were raised to say that not all military operations would lend themselves to blitz tactics, but these were ignored.

Hitler, in particular, was fascinated by the blitz technique, and he heaped praise on Goering so wildly that Goering, who must have known better, never brought up the question of the long-range bomber again in the formative period of the war. Then came the Soviet campaign, which Hitler approached as if it were an extension of the French. But the Soviet front was 1,250 miles long, and in the beginning, as the Soviets retreated, they moved back to the Urals. The Wever Uralbomber was needed, but the Germans did not have it.

The nature of Hitler's Soviet campaign was such that the German army had three main targets, not one as in Poland (Warsaw) or France (Paris). The Germans attacked Leningrad, Moscow and the Caucasus simultaneously. Each target was given the same priority, but the Germans had only one air force in the Soviet campaign, where the technique called for three.

In his planning for the Soviet campaign, Hitler showed no understanding at all of the need for strategic bombing. Indeed, his Directive No. 21, which set up Operation Barbarossa, forbade the use of bombers to hit strategic targets, in connection with the panzer divisions. The Soviet air force was also to be destroyed.

So, as noted earlier, the Luftwaffe went to war in the USSR with insufficient aircraft and the wrong kind of aircraft, and when the Soviets began rapidly producing the tanks and new sort of planes that were needed for this fight, the Germans did not have the aircraft to bomb the factories and the rear areas, and thus the air fighting was all carried out at the troop-support level. At first the German superiority of pilots and planes told, but in the second campaign in the Soviet Union the new generation of fighters and bombers began to make itself felt, while the Germans were still fighting with the aircraft of 1939.

The biggest aircraft the Germans had on the Soviet front was the He-111, which could carry four 1,550-pound bombs.

There were not enough of these, and when the Luftwaffe promised to save Stalingrad for Hitler, those planes were rushed into action as transports. In the Stalingrad campaign alone, 165 of these bombers were lost.

After 1941 it was really too late. By this time Hitler was in serious trouble in the east, and his tactics changed constantly. His one rule was never to surrender any territory on which a German soldier had trod, and from 1942 on he was constantly losing ground but not admitting it. The heavy bombers needed by Germany for support were never forthcoming, and by 1943 the bomber program was a shambles, with the Allies moving fast, coming in with the B-17s, B-24s and Lancaster heavy bombers.

As for air transport, in the early 1930s the Germans simply did not think about air transport. Goering should have, for he was the developer of the German paratroop forces, but he did not understand the concept of transport, and the need for any aircraft different from the bomber. The Japanese were the same: they never developed a proper air-transport service but used twin-engine bombers for transport work. The Germans, called upon to move a large body of troops for Franco during the Spanish civil war, employed the Ju-52 for the job. That was in 1937. The Ju-52 was still the major German transport plane in 1945, although the larger bombers had been pressed into use in the Soviet campaign, with not very good results, because they were prime targets for the new breed of Soviet fighter planes.

So the failure of the Germans to provide a heavy bomber for the Soviet campaign contributed very heavily to the losses, once the Soviets had fallen back and had begun to regroup in the winter of 1942.

Essentially the problem went right to the door of Hermann Goering, who had allowed his responsibility for the whole war effort of the German Reich to keep him from fighting at the proper time for the needs of his own Luftwaffe.

During the first year of the war, the Luftwaffe ran wild, and the air forces of Poland and France were decimated like timber struck by lightning. They suffered heavy losses over the English Channel during the Battle of Dunkirk but still won victory. The euphoria continued until the Battle of Britain. Then it was a different story. The lack of the heavy bomber was felt here for the first time. The Germans set out at first, in July, to destroy the British fighter ability, as noted. By the second week of August the score stood at 148 fighters lost by the British, but to achieve this the Germans had lost 286 planes. In the first two weeks of August the Germans very nearly disabled the British fighter command, but they did not know it and stopped attacking the radar installations just before they had them knocked out. September was the worst month for both sides: the British lost 264 planes and twenty-eight percent of their fighter pilots, and the Germans lost 229 planes and twenty-three percent of their fighter pilots. No air force could stand much of that sort of loss, so the Germans changed strategy, and the blitz of Britain began. Again losses were heavy, and the blitz failed to knock Britain out of the war.

By 1941, the air was more or less a stalemate, expensive to both sides.

When Hitler invaded the Soviet Union, again for the Luftwaffe it seemed remarkably easy. The Soviet aircraft were old and clumsy, and most of them were destroyed on the ground in the air blitz. Indeed, the Luftwaffe estimated that it had destroyed most of the 8,000-plane Soviet force in the first day of fighting. But then the Soviets stopped and reorganized and began bringing out their more modern aircraft, and the air war changed.

With all this, the German air force paid practically no attention to the changes in the enemy's strategy and armament. In 1941 German aircraft production just about equaled Luftwaffe losses. Worse, by the end of German aircraft production, air-crew training had fallen behind. The first note was the shortening of the final training schools' program by a month, in order to get crews into the air. By late winter 1942 the General Staff had lost track of the situation: no one knew how many crews would be available or needed on the various fronts. Every month thereafter the skill level of the new crews decreased.

In 1942 the British began heavy raids on German cities. A thousand planes raided Cologne one night and caused serious damage.

MASSIVE BOMBING

All that Monday, 1 June 1942, the media regaled the nation with tidbits of new information about the great raid. "OVER 1,000 BOMBERS RAID COLOGNE," proclaimed the *Times,* "Biggest Air Attack of the War: 2,000 Tons of Bombs in 40 Minutes."

The flames were higher than I had ever seen before. The buildings were skeletons in the midst of fires. The blast of the bombs was hurling walls themselves across the flames. As we came away we saw more and more of our aircraft below us silhouetted against the flames. I identified Wellingtons, Halifaxes, Manchesters and other Lancasters, lit by the light of the moon. They were doing exactly as we did, going in according to plan, coming out according to plan, and making their way home."

—Charles Whiting, *The Three Star Blitz*

Hitler was up in arms, but the British were unable immediately to repeat the performance, so he forgot about his anger. His attention was focused on the troubles he was having on the Soviet front. In retaliation the Germans launched a series of big raids against British cities. They were called "Baedeker Raids," because the German Air Staff announced that they would go down the list of British cities in the Baedeker guide and knock out each one in turn. The boast did not come to much. Already the failure of the training program had cut into the efficiency of the bombers' crews.

The Luftwaffe could put up a very good fight under certain conditions, as they showed in 1941 and 1942. First was the breakout of the warships *Gneisenau* and *Scharnhorst,* which had been berthed in French ports. The Luftwaffe put up an air screen of 250 fighter planes that prevented the Royal Air Force from getting at the warships. The second big show was Germany's response to the Dieppe raid by the British in August 1942, an attempt to confuse the Germans and to test their English Channel defenses. The raid was a disaster on land and sea. The Luftwaffe came up in force and helped immeasurably with the slaughter of the Canadians. The British lost a destroyer and 106 planes. The Germans lost twenty-one fighters and twenty-seven bombers.

One theater of war in which the Luftwaffe really missed its chance was that of the sea. The combined efforts of U-boats and long-range bombers could be disastrous to shipping, and the British worried a great deal about it—the FW-200, called the Condor, was an especially effective long-range bomber. But Goering did not have much use for the Navy, except U-boats. Although there existed an Atlantic Air Fleet, with eighty-three aircraft, it really never aroused Goering's interest, so a chance was lost. In January 1942, at the height of the sea war, German planes sank twenty ships, while boats sank only twenty-seven. If the Germans had realized the potential, they could have made life much more difficult for the Royal Navy.

In 1942 Hitler did encourage Luftwaffe attacks on the Murmansk convoys and ordered the building of airfields for that purpose in northern Norway. Several convoys were attacked, with excellent results from the German point of view. The Allied convoy PQ-17 lost twenty-three of its thirty-four ships to submarines and aircraft. But again the Germans did not sustain the effort. The Luftwaffe was spread too thin to do so. When the British sent carriers to help the convoys and shot down a large number of attacking aircraft, air attacks on the convoys ceased.

After discovering the dreadful condition of the German aircraft industry in 1941 and removing Ernst Udet from control of technology, General Milch managed to increase aircraft production remarkably, from an average of 981 aircraft per month in 1941 up to 1,296 in 1942, and in December 1942, 1,548 aircraft were produced.

But from 1942, when the Germans were fighting the air war against Britain and the Soviet Union, the air war in the Mediterranean also stepped up. The first real indication of the foolhardiness of Hitler's declaration of war against the U.S. was the Allied landings in North Africa and the concomitant arrival of an American air force, which expanded month after month: as of November 1942 the Luftwaffe was very much on the defensive.

This was also the time when Hitler took over the major decisions.

As noted, Goering made the terrible mistake of promising that he could supply the German Sixth Army at Stalingrad, which he could not do. Further, he interfered in operations in a ridiculous fashion. In December 1942 the Germans lost the air base at Morozovskaya—the reason: the Russians were attacking and came up to within four miles of the airfield with their tanks. When General von Manstein called for all-out Luftwaffe support of the defense, Goering laughed at him. The situation was not nearly so serious, he said. But a few days later the airfield was lost.

Not that Hitler much cared about Goering's support these days. The eastern front was coming apart. Goering agreed with Hitler that no foot of ground must be left uncontested, and this cost the Luftwaffe very heavily in pilots and planes as they supported the losing ground operations. The army generals wanted to establish a bastion along the German frontier and apply all their reserve strength to holding this, but Hitler said no, and Goering as usual supported him. Goering's position with Hitler had virtually collapsed. Stalingrad had fallen largely because Goering could not supply it, or so Hitler said. Actually, Stalingrad had fallen because Hitler would not let General von Paulus retreat from a position that huge Soviet army encirclement had made untenable. But Hitler could never be wrong, and therefore Goering had to be.

That summer Goering's boys did everything they had done before, but the tactics did not work anymore. The Stukas dive-bombed the Soviets, but the Soviet Stormovik fighter bombers hit the transportation centers. The Germans retreated from Kharkov and all along the line. In July and August the 4th and 6th Air Fleets lost a thousand aircraft in the east. But that was not all. The Germans were also fighting in the air in northern Europe and in southern Europe and in the Mediterranean. Total German losses in the three air theaters for those two months were more than three thousand aircraft. There was no way the German aircraft industry could replace that many planes per month.

In the Tunisian campaign the Germans lost 2,500 planes, a defeat which brought about the reorganization of the German air forces in the south, with the 2nd Air Fleet divided into two parts, and General von Richthofen, the expert in ground support, coming from the eastern front to take over command of the 2nd Air Fleet. Adolf Galland, the Luftwaffe's great fighter pilot and commander, took over command of fighters in the Sicilian campaign.

But nothing seemed to help. The eastern Allies kept driving north. Once again the Germans were dogged by Hitler's intransigence. One irrational decision followed another. "Never surrender" became the watchword everywhere, and also the word that was ignored by the ground crews of the Luftwaffe, who had lost faith in their leaders. Field Marshal Kesselring was not much help. He kept reporting to Hitler what Hitler wanted to hear, that things were going to get better. When this did not happen, Kesselring turned almost suicidal. He threatened courts-martial to an air unit that had not given adequate protection to a shipping convoy. He advocated suicide dives of the Japanese sort to his pilots. Hitler thought all this was fine, and so did Goering.

In the summer of 1943 the Allies began dealing devastating blows to Germany from the air. On July 24 came an enormous raid on Hamburg. It was repeated on July 25. On July 26 came a third raid. On July 27 the British staged the greatest raid on Hamburg yet, starting a firestorm that killed perhaps forty thousand people. On July 29 the RAF hit again, and after that the Germans began evacuating the city. Half its buildings were destroyed.

HAMBURG'S HORROR

Horror reveals itself in the howling and raging of the fires, in the hellish din of exploding bombs and in the death-cries of the tormented people. Words fail before the extent of the terror which shook the population for ten days and ten nights. The marks left on the face of the town and of the people can never be erased.

—Hamburg police chief

When Propaganda Minister Goebbels heard the results, he could not believe the devastation was so great. Speer told Hitler that half a dozen such attacks on major cities would bring war production to a halt. Hitler harangued Goering to do something, and Goering did throw more planes into the antibomber defense. For a time the air defenses of the Reich were more formidable.

THE PRICE OF WAR

There was a terrific explosion overhead and the ship rocked badly. A second later the top turret gunner fell through the hatch and slumped to the floor. . . . When I got to him, I saw that his left arm had been blown off at the shoulder and he was a mass of blood.

—American navigator over Hamburg

Then came the great American daylight bombing raids in which hordes of B-17s surged across Europe. But these were unescorted raids. The Germans increased their number of fighters, and the cost to the Americans was high. The German fighters came in tenaciously. But from Goering's point of view, the worst part was yet to come: with the P-47 and the P-38 and finally the P-51 fighter, the Allies could range six hundred miles from base, which put them in reach of almost every German city.

In 1943 Hitler was continually furious, and the target of his fury these days was Goering. All sorts of radical changes were demanded. Hitler wanted the Luftwaffe to concentrate on ground defense (flak guns). Major Hajo Herrmann suggested concentration of day fighters directly over a target to fight night bombing raids, and the use of searchlights to help them. So great was the need that this tactic was used.

But by 1944 the Germans had a shortage of fighters. The Americans were now protecting all their big daylight bombing raids with long-distance fighters. Goering could do nothing. He said the Luftwaffe had to have more fighters, and Hitler agreed. Fighter production was put up to two thousand per month. Milch said it should be five thousand. Now was revealed one of the tragic situations of the war: Hitler came to Goering, and Goering came to Milch and the others, and it became apparent that the Reich Marshal simply did not know what was going on in the Luftwaffe. For three years he had not been paying attention as the war changed. He made the ridiculous statement one day that too much attention was being focused on night fighters!

At the end of 1943 the Western Allies made western Europe the key air theater. The new Allied method was the fighter sweep, which became a more and more common threat that year. The fighters came in great numbers to strike the German airfields and try to knock out the fighters' defenses of the ground. What was needed was greater dispersal. But Goering remained unaware. He wanted more day fight-

BAILING OUT

Then I saw his bombs drop out of the flare of the search-lights, into the darkness, into the depths, into the conflagration. The hideous picture of Hamburg stared me in the face—man-eating lava . . .

. . . I fired; my cannon hammered. I pulled up slightly. Another burst. My heart jumped—I'd hit him! The bomber veered into a steep, diving turn to port. It wasn't burning. I followed it as it continued to dance wildly, until the pilot thought that he had shaken me off.

I closed in, saw streaks of dirt on the aircraft's fuselage, and in the vivid light I saw the rear gunner behind his four guns pointing at me. I aimed and fired into the starboard wing. Again, I heard the dull hammering of my cannon, and my aircraft vibrated, giving me a warm, cleansing feeling of self-fulfillment.

Suddenly, I heard the rattle of bullets against my aircraft. Then emptiness. Silence. My engine had packed in. . . . Smoke began to fill my cockpit. Acrid fumes were coming from somewhere.

I pressed the canopy release and again, harder. . . .

Weightless, I floated away from my faithful Messerschmitt. . . .

For a while I didn't deploy my parachute because I didn't want to spend too long drifting down through the busy, metal-rich airspace.

—Hajo Herrmann, *Eagle's Wings*

ers, but to escort German bombers, not to attack enemy fighters and bombers. He did not see the need for development of a superior fighter. The commitments to the eastern front and to Italy were still all there, demanded by Hitler, but the Luftwaffe was trying to pull together strength to fight in western Europe, and getting trouble from Hitler and Goering at the same time.

The last months of 1943 were terrible for the Luftwaffe chiefs, who watched their organization come apart. Great Allied raids on Schweinfurt, the dams and Peenemünde cost the Allies dearly, but they also cost the Germans fighters. In August, the month of the Schweinfurt raid, the Germans lost 248 fighters.

So great were the disaster and the tension that after the Schweinfurt and Peenemünde raids, Luftwaffe Chief of Staff Jeschonnek put his pistol to his head and killed himself. He was an innocent who had believed in Hitler and Goering until the last.

The major difficulty was that, even after this, Hitler and Goering still did not understand the problem. Milch, who had managed to produce sixty-four percent more planes in 1943 than in 1942, tried to tell them. It made no difference how many planes he produced: losses at the front swallowed all the production.

Milch and his assistants came up with a plan to restructure German air defenses, based on what was known about American aircraft production. Hitler rejected the plan. The Americans could not produce that much, he said.

Hitler returned to one of his favorite themes: fight terror with terror. Germany must have superweapons to destroy the British. And so the total concentration of his mind on air matters turned to the victory weapons, the rockets that would turn the war for him by terrorizing the British into submission. So he believed.

As for Goering, now it was becoming apparent that the technological changes of World War II had completely passed him by. He once told an associate that he did not know how to turn on his own radio. As for radar, once he looked inside a radar receiving set and announced that those little pieces of wire and other things were totally meaningless.

BEHIND THE TIMES

The old fighter pilots of the First World War, who were now sitting at the Supreme Command of the Luftwaffe with Goering at their head, had a compulsory gap of fifteen years behind them, during which they had probably lost contact with the rapid development of aviation.

—General Adolf Galland

In the Reich's labor shortage, Milch suggested that the aircraft industry ought to employ more women, and Goering snorted: the best thing would be give women piecework to do at home while they watched their children.

Milch again suggested that the Germans turn to producing five thousand fighters a month. Goering said it was ridiculous. Hitler agreed.

After Jeschonnek's suicide Günther Korten was made chief of staff, and from this point on, Goering was scarcely consulted at all by Hitler about major Luftwaffe division.

And yet Goering continued to operate. He met his air generals regularly and they reported to him. He toured the fields and kept up morale. He had his uses. The problem was that he had no concept of the force he was commanding and had not had any since his economic duties demanded his full strength midway in the war.

Appearances were deceptive. Goering still commanded the Luftwaffe, no matter how badly, and his word was law. For example, as the Americans brought fighters to escort the bombers, the fighters increased their range with external gas tanks, which they dropped. German pilots, seeing sense in the tactic, began to do the same. Goering was aghast. No pilot was allowed to drop his external tank except under emergency conditions. Not even the Americans would be so wasteful, he assured them.

As the situation of Germany worsened in the air, even Goering, the pragmatist, began to turn toward wonder-weapon tactics to do what common sense said they could not do. Consulting Galland, he issued some new instructions: "The Reich Marshal has ordered the setting up of a *Sturm-staffel* [assault squadron]. Its task will be to break up the enemy by using more heavily armored fighters in all-out attacks. There is no need to discuss here whether this is to be done by shooting down the enemy at the closest range, by employing a new type of weapon or by ramming. . . ." (Harold Faber, *Luftwaffe, a History*)

Goering was coming around to the Hitlerian thesis, also shared by the Japanese, that the moral superiority of the Nazis would more than compensate for the material superiority of the Allies. At the end of 1943 Goering began making public speeches, using this theme, and he even addressed a conference of fighter pilots on the subject. He reproached his pilots for not showing the highest standards of National Socialism—and in this he did indeed give truth to the legend that Germany had "an Imperial navy, Prussian army and Nazi air force."

His audiences were shocked when Goering accused his pilots of cowardice. Hitler often did this, accusing anyone from field marshals down, but for Goering to desert his fighter pilots was something quite new and must have represented his own growing desperation, for he knew that these young men were no more cowards than he had been in World War I.

By the end of 1943 it was apparent in Goering and Hitler's conversation that the high command had no real interest in the air war. Hitler's preoccupation was with the Soviet Union, and a conversation repeated by Goering shows how and why. He and Hitler were talking about air defense of German cities. Hitler said he did not care about air defense of cities. If all the cities were smashed to rubble, that would give people an even more desperate understanding of why they must defeat the Soviets, for the survival of the German people. At first in the war, Hitler had set out on a holy crusade to stamp out Communism. Now he was desperately afraid of what would happen in Germany if the Soviets came in, and his whole strategy was based on this fear. Goering by this time was reduced to saying "Yes, Führer" and very little else.

YES MEN?

Why had he and all the rest of Hitler's followers been such abject "yes men"?

—Dr. Douglas Kelley, psychiatrist

NO MEN

Goering's answer: "Please show me a 'no man' in Germany who is not six feet under the ground today."

As the war worsened, Goering became visibly more concerned, but he was more concerned about the effect on Hitler than anything else. Thus when General Galland, charged with fighter protection, told Hitler to beware that the penetration of American fighters in the Reich would get worse, Goering lost his temper, not unusual in those days.

"What's the idea of telling the Führer that American fighters have penetrated into the territory of the Reich?"

"Herr Reichsmarschall, they will soon be flying even deeper."

"That's nonsense! What gives you these fantasies? That's pure bluff!"

"Those are the facts, *Herr Reichsmarschall.* American fighters have been shot down over Aachen. There is no doubt about it!"

"That is simply not true, Galland. It's impossible."

"You might go there and check it yourself, sir. The downed planes are there on the ground."

"What must have happened was that they were shot down much farther to the west. I mean, if they were very high when they were shot down they could have glided quite a distance before they crashed."

"Glided to the east, sir? If my plane . . ."

Even as the end neared, Goering and Hitler vacillated. And once again Hitler was talking about strategic bombing.

20

DISASTER

Hitler's trust in Goering was eroded not only by Goering's failure to win the Battle of Britain as he had predicted he would, not only by the bombing of Germany, which he had once said would never happen, but by the fall of Stalingrad, which was really not Goering's fault. With all the difficulties of supply, the Luftwaffe might have done it, had not Hitler forced the generals to hold, hold, hold, and thus sacrificed the airfield.

With the fall of Stalingrad in 1943, Hermann Goering's influence with Adolf Hitler hit a new low, from which it never recovered. At the same time the people around Goering had the definite feeling that he no longer had any hope of winning the war. He spoke of new weapons, but even Field Marshal Milch, his main assistant, felt that Goering had no confidence in what he said.

That spring Dr. Goebbels became seriously concerned about Hitler's Russomania and decided to try to organize an inner cabinet to take over the operation of the war. But if this was to work, it needed the full support of Goering, and Albert Speer, who could approach him best, had the definite feeling that he was not enthusiastic about anything. Speer and Goebbels talked Goering around, but not for long.

THE FADING FÜHRER

He too feels that the Führer has aged fifteen years during three and a half years of war.

—Goebbels agreeing with Goering after the Sixth Army defeat

In March the RAF began a series of raids on Berlin, and they destroyed so many houses and killed so many civilians that Hitler was again in a fury.

Goering was searching desperately for some way to turn the tide of the air war. Lieutenant Knöke appeared to find it for him one day in March, shortly after the Führer's latest outbreak of rage.

Knöke had been experimenting with bombs for use by fighter planes against the American B-17s. On March 22 he had the mechanics fix a 500-pound bomb under his fighter, and after a mishap with a blown tire that had to be repaired, he managed to take off and reach an altitude of 22,000 feet. He found a flight of "Fortresses" and stayed above them, away from their deadly fire. Then he fused his bomb, aimed at one plane and let the bomb go. It exploded in the center of a row of Flying Fortresses and broke the wing off one of them. Twenty miles west of Heligoland, the bomber crashed into the sea.

When Knöke came down, he was ordered to report to the commanding officer of his fighter wing, who asked him if he could do it again. He said he thought so, and the air commodore went happily away.

Late that night Knöke had a call from Colonel Henschel. Later he was awakened by a call from a major on Goering's staff, who quizzed him on all the details of his flight and then put him through to the Reich Marshal.

"I am delighted over the initiative you have displayed," said Goering to the lieutenant. "I wanted personally to express to you my particular appreciation."

But, as Knöke knew, the tactic had worked only because of the surprise element, and as soon as the Americans spread the word, the formations opened up and veered off so that the Messerschmitts could not get above them, and the bombing technique tailed off. Once in a while a bomb got a fortress, but Lieutenant Knöke's interceptor squadron shot down many more with gunfire than they destroyed with bombs. By May 1943 Knöke had personally shot down seven Flying Fortresses.

The Luftwaffe did not have enough Knökes. His friend Dieter was shot down one day, and joined Dolenga and Steiger and half a dozen others, only memories in Knöke's dangerous life.

PILOT'S FATALISM

The thought occurs to many of us. "Now when one after the other of the old-timers goes, I can almost reckon by the calendar when my own number will be up."

—Hans Ulrich Rudel, *Stuka Pilot*

In August, his unit was equipped with rockets, and these, again, began to take their toll on the enemy until their effect was partly vitiated when the surprise element wore off and the Superfortress pilots learned how to evade.

As of the autumn of 1943, the handwriting was on the wall, as virtually every Luftwaffe pilot knew. Here is a page from Lieutenant Knöke's life:

> *The Yanks do not leave us alone. Today they attack Münster in strength. Just when I am ready to pounce with my flight on a formation of Fortresses over the burning city, we are intercepted by Thunderbolts (P-47s).*
>
> *A wild dogfight begins. The Thunderbolt has a clumsy appearance which is belied by its high speed and maneuverability. It can still be outfought, however, by a Messerschmitt in the hands of a good pilot.*
>
> *During the dogfight I observe a Messerschmitt 110—one of the aircraft from No. 76 Fighter Bomber Wing—firing four rockets into a group of Fortresses. Two of the Fortresses explode in midair. Thereupon several Thunderbolts come swooping after the victor. Warrant Officers Barran and Führmann and I dive to intercept them.*
>
> *At my first burst of fire a Thunderbolt ahead of me blows up; and Führmann shoots down a second one. That brings the entire pack of Thunderbolts down on our necks. It is all we can do to shake them off. I try every trick I know, and put on quite a display of aerobatics. Finally I get away by spiraling up in a corkscrew climb.*

I know that the Thunderbolt cannot duplicate this maneuver. Unfortunately neither Barran nor Führmann is able to keep up with me. They are still in a serious predicament, with ten or twelve of the Yanks on their tails, and in the meantime the fighter-bombers have got away.

Choosing my time, I return diving into the melee once again, firing at random to divert the attention of our pursuers from Barran and Führmann. In doing so, I am badly hit in the tail plane and left wing where the undercarriage lies retracted.

The crate flips over on its back and plunges down vertically. I am unable to bring it under control again. This infernal dive continues down to 3,000 feet. It is a hell of a sticky situation. I break into a cold sweat all over and my hands begin to shake. "Knöke," I think to myself, "this time you have had it."

In utter desperation I try pushing the stick over to the side. It has jammed. I take my feet off the rudder pedals and in a last resort kick hard against the stick. Suddenly there is a violent jolt, my head is banged hard against the side window, and the plane is back again in normal flying position.

Barran has dived with me but from sheer terror he has remained speechless on the radio.

At Twente I put my aircraft down in a belly landing beside the runway. Half the tail was shot away, and also the right leg from the undercarriage.

Shortly after me a Focke-Wulf comes down to land on the runway. A leg breaks as it touches down on the concrete, it overturns and bursts into flames. The pilot is trapped inside in his seat and burns to death in front of my eyes before he can extricate himself. I am powerless to help: I have to watch him being slowly cremated alive in the wreck. I am trembling at the knees.

A few minutes later a shower of bombs from a formation of heavies comes down close to the airfield.

I have had enough for one day. . . .

And here is Lieutenant Knöke's account of his face-to-face encounter with Reich Marshal Goering, on 17 November 1943. The occasion was the honoring of a number of fighter pilots at Achmer. The pilots, from three wings, were drawn up for inspection. Up came Goering's thirty-car motorcade. The cars stopped and Goering got out to inspect and talk to the pilots.

"Goering makes a most peculiar impression. He wears a unique kind of fancy grey uniform. His cap and epaulettes are covered with gold braid. Bulging legs emerge from scarlet boots of doeskin. The bloated, puffy face makes him look to me like a sick man. Close up I am forced to the conclusion that he uses cosmetics. He has a pleasant voice, however, and is extremely cordial to me. I know that he takes genuine interest in the welfare of his aircrews."

Goering asked the young man about the enemy he had shot down, and was particularly interested in Knöke's first Mosquito bomber. He remembered the occasion because it was one of two Mosquitoes that raided Berlin that night, just as he was making a speech he considered very important. The raid had made him postpone his address for two hours.

After awarding medals, Goering addressed the pilots about the difficulties they were facing. But Knöke had the impression that Goering did not understand the real problem: the technical superiority of the enemy aircraft.

"Such successes as are still being achieved in the face of these overwhelming odds are due solely to the excellent morale and fighting spirit of our aircrews. We need more aircraft, better engines—and fewer headquarters."

In 1943 the Allies began that ten-day series of raids that devastated the important German port of Hamburg. Karl Bodenschatz went to Hamburg to investigate the damage and returned to tell Goering that it had been the worst he had ever seen. If Germany was to save its cities, Bodenschatz said, the Luftwaffe would have to change its tactics and go over to the defense of Germany proper.

Goering held a series of meetings with his senior commanders, and all agreed that this must be the course of action. Specifically the defenses must be gathered around the war industries, to preserve Germany's ability to fight. With some concern, because Hitler had become so changeable in recent months, Goering went to the Führer to report on the decisions of the Luftwaffe and to seek the leader's approval. He came out of Hitler's room a shattered man. General Galland, who was among those waiting for Goering's report, saw how unnerved he was. Goering said that the meeting had been a complete disaster. Hitler had listened to him stonily and then had rejected everything the Luftwaffe leaders had agreed upon. There could be no defensive war. Germany must remain on the offensive.

THE LUFTWAFFE'S LAST CHANCE

The Luftwaffe has disappointed me too often. A change from offensive to defensive in the West is out of the question. I am giving the Luftwaffe its last chance. The air offensive against England must be resumed on a large scale.

—Hitler

And so Goering told his generals, and they told each other that the Führer was absolutely right, and they must go back and strike as many heavy blows against the Americans and the British as they could, and thus prevent their winning the war.

SHOOT-ON-CAPTURE ORDER

In a conference held in May, 1944, attended by Goering and high air force officers, the minutes read as follows: "The Reichsmarschall wishes to propose to the Führer that American and English crews who shoot indiscriminately over towns, at moving civilian trains, or at soldiers hanging on parachutes should be shot immediately at the spot."

—Eugene Davidson, *The Trial of the Germans*

Goering was no longer really a confidant of Hitler's. When the pot boiled over in the east, Goering was not called in. When the Allies landed in Normandy, on 6 June 1944, Goering was not informed for many hours.

But because of Hitler, Goering also quarreled with his generals. They wanted to use the new Me-262, a jet plane capable of 580 mph, as a fighter. And the fighter pilots of Germany approved overwhelmingly. But Hitler decreed, and Goering concurred, that the Me-262 was to be used as a bomber.

Perhaps even the employment of the best weapons and "wonder weapons" would not have turned the tide for the air force. The matter was never really tested, because Hitler's strictures remained on the ground and in the air: never give an inch, he said, and, in obeying, the German forces were decimated and worn down as the war drew toward its close.

On 10 September 1944, Captain Knöke, now a squadron commander, reported that he had been promised replacement planes and pilots for weeks but none had arrived at the Westerwald.

"Here in the Reich the situation has become completely chaotic, ever since Himmler, the Reich Leader of the SS, took over the command of all the Reserve Forces. It would seem that the Führer is transferring the command of the armed services from their own military leaders to his political party bosses. The reputation which Hitler established for himself at the beginning of the war as 'the greatest military genius the world has ever seen' is slowly but surely evaporating. He would do better to leave to his experienced generals the business of conducting the war."

A few days earlier Knöke had joined a conference with General Galland, the chief of the Fighter Command. They talked about disbanding Knöke's squadron altogether, because of the difficulty of bringing it back to strength. Production of aircraft was severely hampered by Allied air raids.

The fuel shortage was almost disastrous. Most of the experienced fighter pilots had been killed or wounded. In the east and in the west, the fronts moved back toward Berlin a little more each day.

Hitler kept talking about secret weapons, but when the first of the new jets came off the line he announced they would be used only for reprisal against the enemy, not in ordinary operations.

Air force men by this time were referring to Hitler's orders as "idiotic," but he rejected every protest, even though the ordinary fighter pilots knew that Galland, Milch and Goering were protesting and getting nowhere.

"The German Fighter Command is slowly bleeding to death," said Knöke. "Our cities and factories are being razed to the ground practically without opposition with deadly precision by the Americans and the British. And the only idea Hitler can think of is 'reprisal.' If we only had one or two wings operating with the new Me-262, there would still be a good chance for the German Fighter Command to save the situation. Otherwise the war in the air will be lost."

The weeks wore on. Captain Knöke, who had survived four years of warfare and shot down fifty-two enemy aircraft, was severely injured in a car accident while moving to a new base. His war ended. He watched from the sidelines as the German air force staged its last big operation on 1 January 1945, in support of the Battle of the Bulge. All the planes that could get aloft in the west bombed and strafed Allied airfields in France and Belgium, and some five hundred German pilots lost their lives. It was all hopeless.

Thereafter the round-the-clock bombing of German cities continued. Knöke watched, some of the time from a slit trench in Friesia.

NO TIME TO BREATHE

The sirens were howling again: the Anglo-Americans were faithfully adhering to their practice of coming back with a second dose before we had time to help the victims of the first. The gang chiefs blew their whistles for retreat. Voices were shouting: "Everyone take cover."

—Guy Sajer, *The Forgotten Soldier*

All during the war the German Luftwaffe was concerned about the problems of fuel supply for aviation—and well they might be. Hitler's "Holy Crusade" against the Soviet Union was not all that holy. Part of it was caused by his hope to secure petroleum supplies from the Caucasus. It did not work: the only oil fields the Germans managed to capture were destroyed by the Soviets before they fled.

In 1943 the German synthetic-fuel program reached its peak. Also, when Germany took Austria she also gained some petroleum resources, and these were increased from 4.2 million tons a year to 7 million tons.

In a way the fall of Italy was a boon, because the Germans no longer had to support Mussolini's oil shortages. And finally, when the Italians quit the war, the Germans took over all the stocks of fuel they could find, and there were a lot of them.

So, surprisingly, for the Germans, in the middle years of the war, fuel was not the problem most people thought it was.

In the spring of 1944 the Eighth and Fifteenth U.S. Air Forces hit the synthetic-fuel industry very hard and created a lot of difficulties. But the German fighters came out in strength and caused many casualties among the American squadrons. Several Allied attacks cut German production temporarily by fifty percent, but within a few weeks it was increased again, almost back to the old levels.

The spring and summer of 1944 were disastrous for the Luftwaffe. The fighting in the air was very fierce, and in April the Eighth Air Force lost more than four thousand planes. But that month the Germans wrote off fifty percent of their front-line fighters. This high rate of attrition meant the training program was cut and cut again. The result was that new German pilots, going into action in 1944, had about half the training given their enemy counterparts.

In the middle of May General Galland came to see Marshal Goering with a new problem, indicative of the devastating nature of the Allied air attack on Germany. So great was the range of the American fighters inside Germany that the Luftwaffe training program was endangered because too often training flights were broken up by American fighter attacks. When added to the operational losses, the figures were devastating. The Reich Air Fleet had lost thirty-eight percent of its pilot strength. In April the Germans had lost 489 pilots, and the training centers had sent up only 396 new pilots.

Galland's suggestions to Goering showed how desperate the situation had become. He wanted all qualified pilots in staff jobs to be put into operational fighter units, all aces now in other jobs to be transferred back to Fighter Command, two groups to be brought from the eastern front to Germany, and some eighty instructors to be taken out of training programs and sent to Fighter Command. Only thus, said Galland, could he keep up with the attrition even for a little while.

The Germans did not know it, but one of their problems

with Allied air superiority was the interception of German Luftwaffe communications by the Allied code breakers using their "Ultra" machine, a copy of the German coding system that was supposed to be foolproof and that the Germans had used all during the war. Because of the Ultra breakthrough, the Allies had been reading Goering's mail for years. On the brink of the invasion of Normandy, the Allies were able to pinpoint the areas of France into which the Germans were moving air units, and then carry out major attacks against them. By June 1 so heavy had been the air attacks that the Germans had no chance to make a major response to the Allied landings.

On 5 June 1944 the 3rd Air Fleet consisted of 815 aircraft, of which 600 were in condition to fight. But the forecasts were for bad weather, and the command made no plans for operations for June 6.

Throughout the night and daylight hours of D-Day the Allies flew 14,000 missions and lost only 127 aircraft.

Field Marshal Sperrle issued an order of the day: "Men of Luftflotte 3! The enemy has launched the long-announced invasion. Long have we waited for this moment, long have we prepared ourselves, both inwardly and on the field of battle, by untiring unending toil. Our task is now to defeat the enemy. I know that each one of you, true to his oath to the colors, will carry out his duties. Great things will be asked of you and you will show the bravest fighting valor."

But the fact was that the 3rd Air Fleet put fewer than a hundred planes into the air, most of them single-engine fighters. That evening the Luftwaffe did slightly better, putting up 175 planes, but Allied troops on the ships and on the beaches noted that few of them even saw a German airplane that day, much less were bothered by one.

The Germans then tried desperately to move air units and

planes into the French region. But the Allied airmen had done a very good job in recent months of interdicting rail transport, and so the movement was dreadfully slow.

Two hundred fighters were moved to reinforce the 3rd Air Fleet within thirty-six hours of the invasion. Another hundred fighters were immediately sent after them.

Goering had ordered a plan for dispersal of fighter units to new fields, and they were all shown the plan, but nothing had been done to make the fields ready for the new units. There were no buildings, no operations towers. There were no communications setups, no protective devices. Between plan and reality there was absolutely no correlation.

Between June 6 and 30 the Allies flew approximately 130,000 missions over the Continent. At the same time the Luftwaffe sorties amounted to 14,000. So the swarms of Allied fighters continued over the beaches day after day. In the first week of operations, the Germans lost 360 planes. In the second week they lost 262. As fast as the Germans sent planes into the Normandy battle, the British and American fighters shot them down.

The Germans tried to give ground support to their troops, but this measure failed because they did not have the proper sort of aircraft for fighter-bomber work. On June 12 they gave up and converted all their fighters back to fighter work. Soon the German fighters were reduced to protecting their own airfields.

The failure of the Luftwaffe was a complete shock to the German soldiers on the ground. They had been told to expect massive retaliation against invasion, and they had. One officer put it this way: "The Führer said that if the invasion came he would send the whole German air force into action at the place of the invasion, even if it meant leaving all forces in all other theaters without air cover."

But when the invasion came, this officer saw one single German plane in the air in three days. The Americans had complete mastery of the air. If his unit tried to move, they were attacked by fighter-bombers. Their petrol supplies were wiped out. They could not move. And there was no Luftwaffe to help them.

From June 6 to 30 the Allied fliers flew 16,000 missions. The 3rd Air Fleet flew 13,000 missions. By June 11 so many German planes had been destroyed that five groups had to be withdrawn from France because of casualties and lost planes.

Another factor in the German failure was Hitler's decision to hold major forces including air forces along the Pas de Calais coast, expecting another invasion there. And the losses continued—so great that Goering personally ordered the squadrons to limit their flights to the absolute minimum.

Then, on 22 June 1944, the Soviets launched a major new offensive against the center of the German line in the east. The German ground forces were thin and nearly exhausted. They began to give ground immediately. The Luftwaffe was of no basic assistance. The Soviet air force now enjoyed a superiority ratio of six to one. Goering rushed a hundred fighters from Italy and fifty from Germany to the east, but losses were so high that overall air strength declined from 2,000 planes in July to 1,700 at the end of the month.

So the Allies in the west drove across France and the Low Countries, and the Allies in the east drove toward Poland, and the Germans could slow them but not stop them. By August 14 the 3rd Air Fleet was down to seventy-five planes.

By the middle of 1944 the Luftwaffe had ceased to exist as a major element of warfare. Its fuel supplies were low. The Allies were now based in France and Belgium. Even the notoriously short-range British Spitfires could cross the

---

LOSING FAITH

The deployment of the *Luftwaffe* to defend against the invasion was a complete failure. Our leadership had failed to recognize the difficulties that faced us, our numerical strength and our state of training. Alternatively they failed to appreciate what was our chance; or they had lost the will and the nerve to take a risk. Inaction sprang from apathy. It was the beginning of the downward path to annihilation.

—Hajo Herrmann, *Eagle's Wings*

Rhine. The Allies kept pounding at the German fuel supply, and on November 2 they staged a massive raid by the Eighth and Fifteenth Air Forces on the German fuel industry. Goering's generals sent up 500 fighters to intercept and lost 123 of them, while shooting down only 40 bombers.

In those last weary months of war, from the end of 1944 until the surrender, the Luftwaffe almost ceased to exist. Indeed, in terms of attrition, it *had* ceased to exist. There was nothing like a tour of operations and then release from combat for the German airman. Consequently the casualty rate was well over ninety percent. Few indeed were the Germans who could say they had survived the entire war in the Luftwaffe. At the end the average length of duty for line pilots was between eight and thirty days. What happened to Captain Knöke was typical—except that by some miracle he survived the war.

The original men of the Luftwaffe were great pilots, no doubt about it. The Germans ran up the greatest list of "kills" of any service. A few of the aces could count their victories in hundreds (Galland totaled 107), but these were the lucky ones who had had good training in the beginning and survived. Only eight of the aces to score over a hundred victories joined the squadrons after 1942. From that point on, the young men who came in were cannon fodder, and most of them lasted a few days or a few weeks.

In January, Goering celebrated his fifty-second birthday at Carinhall, surrounded by his wife Emmy, his sister Olga and his sisters-in-law. They feasted on Russian caviar, duck and pheasant from the local forest, salmon from Danzig and pâté de foie gras from France. There was every wine and every liqueur they could want, including Goering's own Napoleon brandy, which he now kept exclusively for himself.

OUT OF FAVOR

Goering lives a life of idle luxury while the German people suffer. He no longer cares for Germany.

—Hitler

Goering kept coming back to Carinhall that winter, even though the Russians were advancing through his 100,000-acre estate. He kept paratroopers around the place, for protection, until Hitler discovered this and ordered them to Berlin to protect *him*. And then, when it was very late, Goering superintended the loading of a convoy of his favorite things; that done, he said good-bye to everybody who worked on the estate and then pressed a plunger that blew Carinhall to bits.

On April 20, Hitler's birthday, he came up out of the Berlin bunker to meet the faithful, and Goering was there.

During the conversation Goering told Hitler that the last area from north to south through the Bavarian forest was still held by Germans, but that the escape route to Berchtesgaden could be cut at any moment. Hitler retorted with his usual fury of these days that he alone would decide whether to die in Berlin or to try to fight longer in the south.

HITLER HOLDS FAST

How can I call upon the troops to undertake the decisive battle for Berlin if at the same moment I withdraw myself to safety?

—Hitler

After that, Goering approached Hitler privately and said he had urgent tasks waiting in the south and that he would like to leave that very night for Bavaria. Hitler looked at him absently and offered no objection. They shook hands desultorily and Goering left.

GOERING ALONE

I can quite understand why he didn't stay in the bunker, because he hadn't a single friend there. He had only enemies about him.

—Chief of Staff von Greim

Captain Knöke, now an invalid, was ordered to report to the commanding officer of the Wilhelmshaven air station for ground duties. In spite of his crutches, he was kept moving all day, every day, checking fields as possible landing grounds for troop-carrying gliders and making plans for all sorts of impossible defenses. He and other grounded fliers and some forty thousand naval personnel made up the Wilhelmshaven fortress defense, but almost all the naval personnel were inexperienced, and Knöke knew the war was lost.

Down in Obersalzburg, Goering learned on 23 April 1945 that Hitler intended to die in the Berlin bunker. He was told by General Karl Koller, the chief of the Luftwaffe General Staff, who reported from Berlin. So Goering got out a steel box in which he had locked Hitler's decree of 29 June 1941: "If I should be restricted in my freedom of action, or if I should be otherwise incapacitated, Reich Marshal Goering is to be my deputy or successor in all offices of State, Party and Wehrmacht."

That testament seemed very clear, and Goering prepared to act. But first he checked with Berlin, to be sure. The message fell into the hands of Martin Bormann, the secretary who hoped to inherit the Reich, and he lied to Hitler about Goering's intent, and thus infuriated Hitler to the point at which he stripped Goering of his rights of succession and accused him of treason.

ULTIMATUM

Your actions are punishable by death. Because of your valuable services of the past I shall refrain from instituting proceedings if you will voluntarily relinquish all offices and titles, otherwise other steps will have to be taken.

—Hitler

Not knowing, Goering began working on a message to the Allies, as if he were indeed chief of state and the war effort.

Hitler sent back a rocket.

"Decree of 29.6.41 is rescinded by my special instruction. My freedom of action is undisputed. I forbid any move by you in direction indicated."

At the same time, Martin Bormann persuaded Hitler to order the arrest of Goering for high treason by Hans Frank and SS Commander von Bredow in the Berchtesgaden region.

The pair, reinforced by a company of SS men, arrived at the Goering house and surrounded it. They announced to Goering that he was under house arrest. While they were all waiting, the RAF bombed Berchtesgaden, wrecking Hitler's "Eagle's Nest" and also much of the Goering estate.

GRAND DELUSION

Everything will be cleared up by tomorrow. It's simply a matter of a misunderstanding. Sleep peacefully, as I am going to do. Can you imagine for a single moment that Adolf Hitler would have me arrested today—I who have followed him through thick and thin for the last twenty-three years? Come now! It's really unthinkable!

—Goering

After that Goering announced to Hans Frank that he could tell the Führer that if he no longer trusted Goering the Reich Marshal was prepared to be shot. The message was given to Hitler, but Bormann intercepted it and suggested that Goering be shot, and certainly that if Berlin fell he be shot.

"MEN, DO YOUR DUTY"

The situation in Berlin is more tense. If Berlin and we should fall, the traitors of April 23 must be exterminated. Men, do your duty. Your life and honor depend on it.

—Bormann

But Hans Frank knew that the only Nazi in the world who had a possibility of negotiating with the Allies was Goering, so he began to back off from the assignment.

After the bombing Goering suggested they all retire to the safety of Mautendorf Castle, and Frank agreed. They were on their way to the castle when they heard a radio broadcast announce that, "because of ill health," Reich Marshal Goering had been relieved of command of the Luftwaffe. The new commander was Field Marshal Ritter von Greim.

So Goering the mighty, the Iron Man, was now reduced to the rank of ordinary citizen under guard. But when they reached Mautendorf Castle, he sent his niece through some underground passages he knew very well from childhood days to the village below, and she met a Luftwaffe lieutenant. The result was the formation of a rescue operation. It took several days, and in the interim everything in Germany changed.

On April 29 Hitler, prodded by Bormann, stripped Goering of all his titles and honors, and even of his membership in the Nazi party, and appointed Admiral Karl Dönitz his successor. The next day Hitler watched Eva Braun take poison and then he shot himself.

EPITAPH FOR A DICTATOR

It was not cowardly of Hitler to commit suicide. After all, he was chief of the German state. It would be absolutely unthinkable to me to have Hitler sitting in a cell like this waiting trial as a war criminal before a foreign tribunal.
—Goering said later during the trial about Hitler's death

When Goering heard this, he began to behave again as if he had been left heir to the mantle of the Third Reich. He was in touch with Admiral Dönitz, suggesting his course of action. He decided to leave Mautendorf Castle and seek out Eisenhower to negotiate with him. He really believed that the Allies would negotiate, and he did not believe that the demand for unconditional surrender was real.

So the Goering entourage packed up a convoy of goods and furniture and set off to find Eisenhower. They were found, instead, by American Army First Lieutenant Jerome N. Shapiro.

Goering did not see Eisenhower, although the general had promised to see him, but he did see Eisenhower's deputy and chief air officer, General Carl Spaatz. There were unfortunate repercussions to this meeting of Nazis and Americans within the Jewish community and thus within the American political community, so Eisenhower backed away swiftly. Soon Hermann Goering was taken to the U.S. Seventh Army interrogation center at Augsburg, where his medals were taken away, as was the enormous diamond ring he always wore. He was given a living room, bedroom and kitchen but no private bath; he protested, but it did no good.

PLANNING THE END

Goering had suicide much on his mind. He came to his first prison with a vial of cyanide hidden in his navel, secured by an adhesive. It was found and confiscated.

—Eugene Davidson, *The Trial of the Germans*

Hermann Goering was then interrogated, wined, dined and interrogated some more. On May 21 he was moved to a hotel in Luxembourg, where he would spend the next four months.

During this period he was anything but coddled, but one American doctor did help him shake the habit of taking small doses of tranquilizers very frequently—a habit, but not a "drug habit" in the normal sense of the words and no more serious than cigarette smoking. He lost eighty pounds and was a trim two hundred pounds when he was transferred to Nuremberg Prison for the war-crimes trials being held by the Allies.

GOERING CAGED

Goering was delivered to Nuremberg jail in September 1945. The cell in which he spent the last year of his life has been described often enough. It was 9 feet wide and 13 feet long, approached by a thick wooden door which faced a barred window set high in the opposite wall. The furniture was simple.

—Ewan Butler and Gordon Young,
The Life and Death of Hermann Goering

Goering knew from the beginning that the trials were a show and that he was certain of conviction and hanging.

"Yes, I know I shall hang. You know I shall hang. I am ready," he told Dr. Kelley.

From Goering's point of view, there was only one important aspect to what he called the victor's justice to which he was subjected. It would give him a chance to make a record for the German people.

"I am determined to go down in German history as a great man. If I cannot convince the court, I shall at least convince the German people that all I did was done for the Greater German Reich. In fifty or sixty years there will be statues of Hermann Goering all over Germany."

The Nuremberg war-crimes trials. Victor's justice. What else would one expect?

THE JUDGMENT OF HISTORY

The victor will always be the judge and the vanquished the accused.

—Goering

But having said that, one must also say that the International Tribunal did give the defendants every chance to cross-examine witnesses and to expound their own activities. The purpose of the prosecutors and the tribunal was to make a record for the world that would show future generations and the German people of the war generation just what sort of government had been in power from 1934 until 1945.

Hermann Goering saw in the war-crimes trials his own chance to show how he regarded his role in history. He set out to do that.

HIS LAST STAND

Goering was convinced that such defense as he needed could well be supplied from his capacious and extremely accurate memory. From his point of view this trial had only one purpose—that he might appear in Court as the Führer, the last great representative of National Socialism, and there expound his creed, so that his words might go down in German history and the Nazi legend might live.

—Ewan Butler and Gordon Young,
The Life and Death of Hermann Goering

The indictment was read out on 20 November 1945, and for the next 120 days Allied prosecutors conducted their trial.

ACCUSED BY THE WORLD

Goering was charged at Nuremberg on four counts: he had plotted to wage aggressive warfare; he had waged it; he had committed war crimes; he had committed crimes against humanity. He was universally considered guilty from the outset and appeared on all the lists of war criminals.

—Eugene Davidson, *The Trial of the Germans*

TO FACE THE ENEMY

What is there to be afraid of? After I have given orders to hundreds of thousands of men to go into battle, frequently knowing full well that many would not come back, plain soldiers who had no choice in the matter, should I, their leader, cringe when called on to face the enemy?

—Goering

As the defendants gathered to plan their joint defense against the charges brought, it was apparent that Goering was their leader. It was also apparent that he was an unrepentant Nazi. He quarreled with Albert Speer over Hitler, and from that point on, they fought for the allegiance of the other defendants. By February 15, the prison authorities were convinced by Speer that Goering had too much influence on the other prisoners, so they were all once more reduced to solitary confinement. Thereafter the prison authorities kept devising new methods to isolate Goering from the other defendants and thus prevent him from influencing them.

Goering put up a stout defense for himself.

Witnesses testified that he had worked for peace and had tried first to prevent and then to stop the war, that he had helped people who got in trouble with the Gestapo and other government agencies and that he had treated his enemies very well.

When his case was brought up he was ready, and for four days relived the days of National Socialism in Germany with almost total recall of events, personalities, places, times and conversations. It was like having a camera on the events.

GOERING'S DEFENSE

The Führer, Adolf Hitler, is dead. I was regarded as his successor in leading the German Reich. Consequently . . . I acknowledge my responsibility for having done everything to carry out the preparations for the seizure of power and to make that power firm in order to make Germany free and great. I did everything to avoid this war, but after it had started my duty was to do everything to win it.

—Goering

WITHOUT SHAME

During the trial Goering made no attempt, as did so many of his co-defendants, to place the blame on others or to hide behind the corpse of Hitler. On the contrary, he strove to emphasize the significance of his own role in the Reich.

—Eugene Davidson, *The Trial of the Germans*

Goering made an impressive case for the Nazis, the principle of National Socialism and of dictatorship. He decried Gestapo excesses and said he had opposed them at the time. One of the judges, Britain's Sir Norman Birkett, wrote about Goering's performance:

Goering is the man who has really dominated the proceedings and that, remarkable enough, without ever uttering a word in public up to the moment he went into the witness box.

> *That in itself is a very remarkable achievement,
> and illuminates much that was obscure in the past
> few years. He has followed the evidence with great
> intensity when the evidence required attention,
> and has slept like a child when it did not, and it has
> been obvious that a personality of outstanding
> though possibly evil qualities was seated there in
> the dock. No one seems to have been quite pre-
> pared for his immense ability and knowledge and
> his thorough mastery and understanding of the
> detail of the captured documents. He has obvi-
> ously studied them with the greatest care and ap-
> preciated the matters which might assume the
> deadliest form.*

No one on the Allied side quite liked all this, and they
hoped that in cross-examination American Supreme Court
Justice Robert H. Jackson would destroy the impression that
Goering had left.

"HALF MILITANT AND HALF GANGSTER"

[He] was half militant and half gangster. He stuck a pudgy
finger in every pie. —He was equally adept at massacring
opponents and at framing scandals to get rid of stubborn
generals. He built up the *Luftwaffe* and hurled it at his
defenseless neighbors. He was among the foremost in harrying the Jews out of the land. If you were to say of these
men that they are not guilty, it would be as true to say that
there has been no war, there are no slain, there has been
no crime.

—Justice Robert H. Jackson, U.S. chief prosecutor

But this did not happen. Justice Jackson was not familiar with German history, and so Goering had many opportunities to make what were really speeches on historical matters, and always, of course, they favored his point of view.

Then, instead of destroying the self-picture that Goering had presented in testimony, the cross-examination strengthened it and showed him to be a friend to Jews, an opponent of the war with the USSR, and a loyal subject to Hitler. It also destroyed the anti-Goering myth that he had set the Reichstag fire himself.

LOYAL TO THE END

I am here neither to justify the Führer, Adolf Hitler, nor to glorify him. I am here only to emphasize that I remained faithful to him, for I believe in keeping one's oath not in good times only but also in bad times, when it is much more difficult.

—Goering

The cross-examination ended on 22 August 1946. Then came the questioning of others, and four long months went by until the summations began. Then more verbiage, and finally, on August 31, each of the prisoners was allowed to make a last speech.

Goering denied everything.

"I never decreed the murder of a single individual at any time, nor decreed any other atrocities, nor tolerated them while I had the power and the knowledge to prevent them. I did not want war nor did I bring it about. I did everything to prevent it by negotiating. After it had broken out, I did everything to assure victory. The only motive which guided me was my ardent love for my people and my desire for their happiness and freedoms. And for this I call on the Almighty and my German people as witnesses."

"LET THE PEOPLE FORGET"

No, none of them must go down in history as the least bit worthy of respect. Let the whole damn Nazi system and all who participated in it, including myself, go down with the ignominy and disgrace it deserves. And let the people forget and start to build a new life on some sensible democratic basis.

—Speer

But the speeches really made no difference to the proceedings. On 30 September 1946, Goering was found guilty of a whole list of war crimes, dating back to the organization of the Nazi party, slave labor, persecution of the Jews. He was found to have been the leading war aggressor, second only to Hitler. Hjalmar Schacht, Franz von Papen and Hans Fritsche got off, but the others were all sentenced, and Goering was to hang.

He asked for death by firing squad—a soldier's end—and was refused. And so the drama had been played out, almost until that last few hours, when Hermann Goering once more fooled his enemies and cheated them of their revenge.

GUILTY

Hermann Wilhelm Goering, on the counts of the indictment on which you have been convicted, the International Military Tribunal sentences you to death by hanging.
                —Lord Justice Lawrence, Presiding Judge

The executions were planned for 16 October 1946. On the evening of October 15 the chaplains made the rounds of the cells of the condemned, and one visited Goering. He seemed downcast but composed. The chaplain left, the guards came back on duty, and the prison quieted down, the officials waiting for 2:00 A.M., when the executions would begin.

FACING GOD

Pastor, I believe in God. I believe He watches over the affairs of men. But only the big ones. He is too great to bother about little matters like what becomes of Hermann Goering.
                —Goering

The guards watched. Goering seemed to sleep, or at least to rest, moving his hands around his body as a person does. But then the personal guard detailed to watch his cell saw the Reich Marshal's body stiffen and make a choking sound. When they opened the cell and rushed in, the doctor found him dead.

GALLOWS AND ASHES

At 2:00 A.M. on October 16, 1946, Joachim von Ribbentrop took Goering's place as the first Nazi leader to die on the gallows in the gymnasium of Nuremberg jail. Wilhelm Keitel followed, and then Kaltenbrunner, Rosenberg, Frank, Frick, Streicher, Jodl and Seyss-Inquart. At 3:15 A.M., it was all over. The cremations began immediately and continued all day.

When they were finished, a car drew up at the crematorium and a container with the ashes in it was placed aboard. It was still raining. The car set off into the countryside. An hour later . . . the charred remains of the lords of the Third Reich, Hermann Goering's among them, were poured out into the muddy gutter.

—Leonard Mosley, *Reich Marshal*

EPILOGUE

Half a century after Hermann Goering cheated the hangman, he remains the most interesting figure of the Third
Reich. One of my editors suggested that I seem to show a
certain sympathy for Goering. If that is true, it is quite
inadvertent; to my mind, Goering, who did not believe in the
racist precepts of Nazism, was by his own statements the
most dastardly of all the major Nazi leaders. Goering was
"golden boy," the model of Aryanism: blond, tall, handsome, devil-may-care; with a bright smile and a glance for
every girl, he was the Wunderkind—the prodigy. Even at his
most outrageous, in his Reich Marshal rig, with a baton and
dripping with medals like a Central American dictator,
Goering had style. It is Goering as a war leader of the Third
Reich that I have examined, in the pattern of my *Hitler's
War*.

It is curious that even as the war began, Hitler took on ever
more military power, and Goering lost it to him until at the
end Hitler was running the air force as well as the army, and
Goering was reduced to economic master of what was left of
the Greater Reich. He was a soldier, and a very good one,
during World War I: the German Flying Corps, in particu-

lar, was heaven-sent for a shocked young Goering who saw the German officer corps flinging the past to the winds with their medals and advocating a soviet within the army in 1919 and 1920. It denied everything he had fought for, and it is clear that Goering saw in Hitler a man capable of doing what they both thought had to be done for Germany. By the 1930s Goering could give Hitler an entrée into the moneyed circles of Germany, which Goering had been cultivating while Hitler was in jail. It took a peculiar combination of businessman and war hero—never forget the value of the Pour le Mérite to the upper class—which, in the circle around Hitler, only Goering possessed. In return Hitler gave him power.

In those frantic struggles for position in the 1930s Goering guessed right time after time. Conceivably he might have sided with Röhm against Hitler, but he knew Röhm well and he knew Hitler better. When Himmler and Heydrich wormed their way into Goering's province and took charge of it, Goering's answer was to find for himself a new niche, that of economic boss; for Hitler had relied on the conservatives who owned German capital, but had always been uneasy with the alliance, and by 1935, when he had the power, he began to move away from it; so that when Goering found that Hitler no longer trusted Hjalmar Schacht and his consortium of bankers and industrialists, he found himself "economic tsar." Hitler was, after all, a real radical of the right, and he hated capitalists.

During the 1930s British visitors to Germany were captivated by Goering. He could make a reasoned case for National Socialism, pointing out the easy way in which it worked with the Ruhr industrialists and the German bankers; but the truth was that in the middle 1930s, when Goering was assembling his industrial empire in the Third Reich, he was also disassembling German capitalism, and in the end of the Reichswerke Hermann Goering was a fitting monument to Nazi economics: total control by the state.

But Goering's activities were conducted on a grander scale. He began in 1938 to woo the British ambassador with lavish entertainment and stag hunts at Carinhall. He offered to go to Britain and personally negotiate a settlement to German-British differences. And when all failed, despite Hitler and Goering's conviction that Britain would not fight, and Britain did go to war, Goering turned quickly. His was the idea of bringing Britain to her knees by terror attack after the RAF had withstood the Battle of Britain. When the Germans invaded the Soviet Union, Goering immediately accepted Hitler's policy of starvation and murder, relaxing the murder only when the industrial leaders of the Third Reich intervened, needing manpower for their factories; there was never any indication that he did it on humanitarian grounds.

In his detailed study, R. J. Overy concluded that Goering developed a set of political principles matching those of Hitler, probably in the period of his isolation in Italy and Sweden. Perhaps he did; but he certainly gave no indication of it afterward. His career was marked by rapid change in direction to fit circumstances. When elected to the Reichstag, for example, as much because of his social contacts and his war-hero stature as because of Nazi political support, Goering showed Hitler that the war hero had the public respectability that Hitler himself had never sought. Thus in the Reichstag Goering was a tactician, not a strategist. He was the politician, the man who knew how to get things done. So Hitler appointed Goering chief of the Sturmabteilung in 1922 because it was an excellent public-relations gesture.

As progenitor and leader of the Luftwaffe, too, he was the organizational genius. From General Ludendorff he adapted the concept of total war to the Luftwaffe. He put the air force together and within two years had it functioning well enough to try out the results in the Spanish civil war, with remarkable effect. German air might in Spain was superior to that of Mussolini and to that of the Soviets, who sent pilots and planes to the other side. Goering persuaded Erhard Milch to leave civil aviation and head the military arm as his deputy. He made Walther Wever chief of staff; a brilliant appointment, for Wever was a dedicated airman who saw the future. He employed Ernst Udet when daring and new ideas were needed. But then, having started the organization and provided the money and the grandeur of the ministry's Berlin establishment, typically he turned his attention elsewhere. His whole approach to military aviation was to rely on his experience of the past, not to plan for the future. He had no time; he was too busy as minister, as Hitler's deputy, adviser and personal diplomatic envoy, too busy plotting the downfall of Austria, too busy taking over the economic control of the Reich from the bankers, to devote the time necessary to changing the air world. Consequently, by the time the war began in 1939, Goering was out of touch with military developments, and he never recovered. Had Goering been close to his Luftwaffe staff when Wever died in 1936, he would have known that General Albert Kesselring was not the right man for the job. But by 1936 Hitler had put Goering in charge of the entire Reich economy and he was engaged in the tournament of power with Hjalmar Schacht.

It is clear that when Hitler launched the campaign against Russia, his generals knew that his purpose was the utter destruction of the Soviet state and the subjugation of the Soviet people. Goering was under no misapprehensions. He told one of his generals that when Soviets were captured every Bolshevik functionary should be shot without any sort of trial.

Hitler gave him the resolution of the problems of economy and race encountered in the conquered countries, and he was an avid supporter of Hitler's final solutions to the Soviet and Polish and Jewish problems.

At the Nuremberg trials Goering indicated that he had opposed the war with the Soviet Union. Such a claim seems false, based on the records. If he did not want that war, he did precious little to stop it.

One would think that, as heir apparent to control of the Nazi party, Goering would have developed a personal following and a power base, but his apparent power depended entirely on Hitler's favor. Goebbels and Bormann were both much more secure in the party structure than Goering ever became. He crucially failed to make a major impact with the *Gauleiters,* the local party leaders, for example; when Goering went back to Bavaria at the end he was arrested through a local *Gauleiter.*

But Goering had lost Hitler's confidence long before this, largely through the failure of the Luftwaffe to work miracles in the eastern war. Thus, when the building genius Fritz Todt died in a plane crash, in February 1942, Goering, who sought to consolidate his control over the German economy by taking on Todt's duties, was rebuffed by Hitler, and Albert Speer became the wonder boy of the Third Reich. Goering had assured Hitler that he could destroy the Soviet air force, and he had not. So Speer became minister of armaments and head of wartime construction, and these proved to be the key economic posts of the war's last years. The death of Todt signaled the decline of Goering. Theoretically he still controlled Germany's economy. Actually Hitler controlled it himself, through Speer, for although Speer was minister of armaments, on 2 April 1942 Hitler decreed that only his own Oberkommando Wehrmacht (Army High Command, now under the personal control of Hitler) could issue orders for armaments, and by 1943 Goering was virtually in isolation within the party and within the Reich. Most of his time was spent at Carinhall, where he surrounded himself with a select circle, mostly young people, whom his senior Luftwaffe staff referred to bitingly as *"das Kindergarten"*—"the nursery." In the last two years, Goering was quite outside the circle of Hitler intimates. This was inevitable. While Hitler in the flush of success of 1934 had created him as "successor," it was apparent to Goering as early as 1942 that there would be no successor and no "Thousand-Year Reich." After 1942 his constant pronouncement was that the war was lost. So in the last months, Goering simply marked time and waited for the end, until that fateful day in 1946 when the hangman called; and Hermann Goering, in taking his own life, left this world with a dignity he had not enjoyed while in it.

THE DECISION TO DIE

After careful consideration and heartfelt prayers to God, I have decided, rather than to allow my enemies to hang me, to kill myself. I would at any time accept death by shooting. But the hanging of Germany's Reich Marshal cannot be allowed.

—Goering in letter to wife

BIBLIOGRAPHIC NOTES

I am indebted to the U.S. Library of Congress for bibliographical materials and to the Bundesarchiv of the German Federal Republic, at Freiburg, for materials on Goering's career, and particularly to Dr. Granier there.

Bewley, C. H. *Hermann Goering and the Third Reich.* New York: Devlin Adair, 1962.

Boddeker, Günther. *Die Kapsel d. Deheimnis um Görings Tod.* Düsseldorf: Rudiger Winter, 1979.

Butler, Ewan. *Marshal Without Glory.* London: Tandem, 1973.

Butler, Ewan and Gordon Young. *The Life and Death of Hermann Goering.* California: Borgo Press, 1990.

Davidson, Eugene. *The Trial of the Germans.* New York: Macmillan, 1966.

Faber Harold, ed. *Luftwaffe, A History.* New York: Times Books, 1977.

Fontander, Bjorn. *Goering och scerige.* Stockholm: Raben & Sjogren, 1984.

Frischauer, Willi. *Goering.* London: Odham's Press, undated.

Gutzbach, Erich. *Hermann Goering*. London: Hurst & Blackett, 1939.

Herrmann, Hajo. *Eagle's Wings*. Wisconsin: Motorbooks International, 1991.

Knöke, Hans. *I Flew for the Führer: The Story of a German Airman*. Translated by John Ewing. 2d ed. London: Evans Brothers, 1979.

Lange, Eitel. *Der Reichsmarschal im Kriege*. Stuttgart: C. E. Schwab, 1950.

Lee, Asher. *Goering: Air Leader*. New York: Ballantine Books, 1972.

Manvell, Roger. *Hermann Goering*. London: New English Library, 1968.

Mosley, Leonard. *Reich Marshal*. New York: Doubleday, 1974.

Murray, Williamson. *Luftwaffe*. London: George Allen & Unwin, 1985.

Overy, R. J. *Goering, the Iron Man*. London: Routledge & Kegan Paul, 1984.

Paul, Wolfgang. *Wer War Hermann Goering?* Esslingen: Bechtle, 1983.

Rudel, Hans Ulrich. *Stuka Pilot*. California: Noontide Press, 1987.

Sajer, Guy. *The Forgotten Soldier*. New York: Brassey's (US) 1990.

Shirer, William L. *The Rise and Fall of the Third Reich: A History of Nazi Germany*. London: Secker and Warburg, 1960.

Skipper, G. C. *Goering and the Luftwaffe*. Chicago: Children's Press, 1980.

Sommerfeldt, Martin H. *Hermann Goering, Ein Lebensbild*. Berlin: Mittler & Sohn, 1934.

Swearingen, Ben E. *The Mystery of Hermann Goering's Suicide.* London: Robert Hale, 1986.

Townsend, Peter. *The Odds Against Us.* New York: Zebra, 1988.

Whiting, Charles. *The Three Star Blitz.* London: Leo Cooper Ltd., 1987.

Nuremberg Trial of major German war criminals, 1945–6

INDEX

In accordance with the German style all proper names with "von" are indexed under the letter "v"—thus "Joachim von Ribbentrop" is listed as "von Ribbentrop, Joachim" instead of "Ribbentrop, Joachim von."